CARL SCHMITT TODAY

Originally published as *Carl Schmitt actuel: Guerre 'juste,' terrorisme, état d'urgence, 'Nomos de la terre'* (Paris: Éditions Krisis, 2007).

First English edition published in 2013 by Arktos Media Ltd.

Copyright © 2013 by Arktos Media Ltd.

Published in the United Kingdom.

ISBN 978-1-907166-39-6

BIC classification:
Social & political philosophy (HPS)
Afghan War (HBWS4)

Translation: Alexander Jacob
Editors: Tobias Ridderstråle and John B. Morgan
Cover Design and Layout: Daniel Friberg
Proofreader: F. Roger Devlin, Ph.D.

ARKTOS MEDIA LTD
www.arktos.com

Alain de Benoist

Carl Schmitt Today

Terrorism, 'Just' War, and the State of Emergency

ARKTOS
London, 2013

TABLE OF CONTENTS

A NOTE FROM THE EDITOR

The original edition of this book was published in French in 2007, so references to the contemporary American government are to the administration of George W. Bush. Unless otherwise indicated, the footnotes to the text were added by the author himself in the original edition. Additional footnotes which were added by the editors or the translator for this edition are so marked. Where sources in other languages have been cited, I have attempted to replace them with existing English-language editions. Citations to works for which I could locate no translation are retained in their original language. Web site addresses for on-line sources were verified as accurate and available during April 2013.

I would like to thank Dr. F. Roger Devlin for his careful proofreading of the manuscript, which made many significant improvements to it.

JOHN B. MORGAN
Panaji, Goa, India
29 April 2013

Introduction: 'Just War,' Terrorism, State of Emergency, 'The Nomos of the Earth'

Many works have been published these last years on the influence, real or supposed, of the American philosopher of German origin Leo Strauss (1899-1973) on the American 'neoconservative' milieu.[1] According to an opinion expressed rather frequently, it was due to contact with or reading the works of Strauss that the majority of neoconservatives became convinced of the excellence of democracy (confused by them with the capitalist system), of the 'universal' validity of the principles that they profess and of the necessity of exporting them all over the world, by force if necessary. Alain Franchon and Daniel Vernet thus write that 'by derivation or by capillary action [...] the philosophy of Strauss has served as a theoretical basis for neoconservatism.'[2] The thought of Strauss is said to be the 'background' to the actions of the partisans of George W. Bush. The proof

---

1 Cf., notably, Shadia B. Drury, *Leo Strauss and the American Right* (New York: St. Martin's Press, 1997). By the same author: *Political Ideas of Leo Strauss* (London: MacMillan, 1988); 'Leo Strauss e i neoconservatori,' *Iride*, XVII, 42, May-August 2004, pp. 291-301; 'La sponda americana: un modello politico? Sterminare il nemico. Leo Strauss e Carl Schmitt,' *Il Ponte*, 2-3 (2005), pp. 103-117. The best study on the influence of Strauss on the United States remains, however, that of Kenneth L. Deutsch and John A. Murley (ed.), *Leo Strauss, the Straussians, and the American Regime* (Lanham: Rowman & Littlefield, 1999). The thesis of an influence of Leo Strauss on the neoconservatives has also been repeated recently in a more summary, if not simplistic, manner, by Anne Norton, *Leo Strauss and the Politics of American Empire* (New Haven: Yale University Press 2004). Cf. also Benjamin Barber, 'Among the Straussians,' *The New York Review of Books*, 14 April 1988; Alfons Söllner, 'Leo Strauss. German Origin and American Impact,' in Peter Kielmansegg, Horst Mewes and Elisabeth Glaser-Schmidt (eds.), *Hannah Arendt and Leo Strauss* (New York: Cambridge University Press, 1995), pp. 121-137; and William Pfaff, 'The Long Reach of Leo Strauss,' *International Herald Tribune*, 15 May 2003. A measured formulation: Edward Skidelsky, 'No More Heroes,' *Prospect*, March 2006, pp. 34-37.

2 Alain Franchon et Daniel Vernet, 'Le stratège et le philosophe,' *Le Monde*, 16 April 2003. Cf. also Heinrich August Winkler, 'Wenn die Macht Recht spricht,' *Die Zeit*, 18 June 2003.

is the critique of relativism conducted in the entourage of the latter, its frequent recourse to moral vocabulary, its insistence on 'values,' and so forth.

This influence was said to have been exercised, notably through the intermediary of Allan Bloom, Harvey Mansfield, Harry Jaffa or Albert Wohlstetter, on Paul D. Wolfowitz, William Kristol, Robert Kagan and Donald Rumsfeld, all four members of the Project for the New American Century, but also on men as diverse as William Bennett, Elliot Abrams, Richard Perle, Michael Novak, Norman Podhoretz, Dick Cheney, Michael Ledeen, Charles Krauthammer, Gary Schmitt, Zalmay Khaizad, Alan Kayes, Francis Fukuyama, John Ashcroft, Samuel Huntington, Clarence Thomas, Robert Bork, Leon Kass, Harvey Mansfield, Lewis Libby, and many more. 'Straussian' foundations are also named in this context, such as the Lynde and Harry Bradley Foundation.

An intellectual affiliation between Leo Strauss and the principal members or partisans of the present government of the United States has sometimes been claimed by certain neoconservatives themselves.[3] It has nevertheless been equally disputed, not only because Leo Strauss could obviously not be held responsible for the policies implemented by some of his readers or disciples — and, in any case, nobody can know how he himself would have judged the present orientations of the White House — but also because his political thought, which was essentially philosophical in nature, diverges from the neoconservative ideology on important points.[4] Strauss' daughter has disputed the idea

---

3   Cf. Carnes Lord, 'Thoughts on Strauss and Our Present Discontents,' in Kenneth L. Deutsch and John A. Murley (eds.), *Leo Strauss, the Straussians, and the American Regime,* op. cit.; Steven Lenzner and William Kristol, 'What Was Leo Strauss Up To?,' *The Public Interest,* Fall 2003.

4   Cf., on this point, notably, Carole Widmaier, 'Leo Strauss est-il néoconservateur ? L'épreuve des textes,' in *Esprit,* November 2003, pp. 23-38. Widmaier contests that the thought of Strauss can be approximated to a political theory or that it is the thought of a particular culture (that of American democracy). The Straussian ethic, she says, 'is not that of politics, but that of thought' and more especially that of a strictly philosophical thought. Emphasizing in passing that the use that the neoconservatives make of the term 'values' strongly differs from that which Leo Strauss made of it, she thinks that 'the messianism tinted with optimism of the neoconservatives is absent from the thought of Strauss' and that 'the designation of an 'axis of evil' is, in spite of its appearances, properly *anti-Straussian.*' She concludes that 'the neoconservative interpretation of the ideas of Strauss is not really that: it is a matter, more or less, of a betrayal' (p. 36) and that the 'object of Strauss is not politics but *philosophy*' (p. 38). Cf. also Laurence Berns, 'Correcting the Record on Leo Strauss,' *Political Science and Politics,* XXVIII, 4 (December 1995); Heinrich

that her father was ever 'the mastermind behind the neoconservative ideologues who control United States foreign policy.'[5] Besides, Leo Strauss, a notoriously anti-historicist philosopher,[6] never referred to international questions in his books and, in a more general way, had only very rarely made statements on contemporary questions. But our intention is not to settle this point. It is rather to appreciate the manner in which, from 2003, an entire polemic has developed which, with reference to the actions of the neoconservatives, has closely associated the names of Leo Strauss and Carl Schmitt.

These polemics, the origins of which coincided with the thirtieth anniversary of the death of Leo Strauss, essentially aimed at discrediting the neoconservative milieus of which Strauss was said to be the 'guru,' by making him seem to endorse views attributed to Carl Schmitt. The general idea was that Schmitt was said to be a 'Nazi' thinker, that Leo Strauss, Schmitt's accomplice, propagated in his turn the same 'Nazi' ideas in America, and that the George W. Bush administration, influenced by the thought of Leo Strauss, was linked by this intermediary to the ideas of Schmitt and thus to Nazism. This grotesque thesis has frequently been accompanied by a quasi-conspiratorial representation of Straussian thought, which was said to be informed by 'esoteric' considerations and inspired by strategies aimed at placing near the people in power more or less cynical 'philosophical

---

Meier, 'Der Philosoph der Stunde,' *Focus*, 30 June 2003, pp. 54-57; Thomas G. West, 'Que dirait Léo Strauss de la politique étrangère américaine?,' *Commentaire*, Spring 2004, pp. 71-78; and Mark Lilla, 'Leo Strauss: The European,' in *The New York Review of Books*, 21 October 2004, pp. 58-60, which makes us note that there are fewer 'Straussians' around George W. Bush than there were in the administrations of Ronald Reagan and George Bush, Sr. Two other more recent works: Heinrich Meier, 'Pourquoi Leo Strauss? Heurs et malheurs de l'école pour la vie philosophique,' *Commentaire*, Summer 2006, pp. 307-313; and, especially, Daniel Tanguay, 'Néoconservatisme et religion démocratique: Leo Strauss et l'Amérique,' ibid., pp. 315-324. 'It would be an error,' writes the latter, 'to believe that the Straussian themes have been transposed without modification into the neoconservative political discourse. Their political adaptation was a complex task and it caused these themes to undergo profound modifications, sometimes going so far as to affect the original meaning' (p. 317). 'The extreme polarisation of Strauss by his American disciples and the neoconservatives,' he adds, 'risks obscuring the orientation of the movement of the thought of Strauss' (p. 322).

5 Jenny Strauss Clay, 'The Real Leo Strauss,' in *The New York Times*, 7 June 2003.

6 For a critique of Straussian anti-historicism, cf. Claes G. Ryn, 'History and the Moral Order,' in Francis Canavan (ed.), *The Ethical Dimension of Political Life* (Durham: Duke University Press, 1983); and Paul Gottfried, *The Search for Historical Meaning* (DeKalb: Northern Illinois University Press, 1986).

advisors' working towards secret objectives. Leo Strauss has thus been accused of having recommended lies and duplicity to politicians by considering that the truth should be reserved to an elite, which has allowed him to be denounced as a 'fascist' (by Glen Yeadon). In all cases, it was a matter of making use of some of the critiques to which Schmitt had been subjected, owing to the fact of his compromise with the Nazi regime (between 1933 and 1936) to discredit, first Leo Strauss, and, through him, his supposed disciples, all being henceforth suspected of 'Nazi' opinions or practices.

This thesis was first expressed in the public press by a few isolated authors[7] before being repeated systematically, in a still more polemical manner, in circles close to the very controversial Lyndon B. LaRouche.[8] It then appeared in the most diverse milieus. Particularly significant is the article of the former dean of the faculty of Political Science at the

---

7   Cf. James Atlas, 'A Classicist's Legacy: New Empire Builders,' *The New York Times*, 4 May 2003; and Seymour Hersh, *The New Yorker*, 5 May 2003. Cf. also three articles which appeared some years earlier: Hiram Caton, 'Explaining the Nazis: Leo Strauss Today,' *Quadrant*, October 1986, pp. 61-65; Jacob Weisberg, 'The Cult of Leo Strauss: An Obscure Philosopher's Washington Disciples,' *Newsweek*, 3 August 1987; and Brent Staples, 'Undemocratic Vistas: The Sinister Vogue of Leo Strauss,' *The New York Times*, 28 November 1994.

8   To better 'nazify' the American neoconservative milieus (practising thus what Leo Strauss himself called the '*reductio ad hitlerum*') the partisans of LaRouche have not hesitated to resort to the most extravagant statements expressed in terms which are not only outrageous but sometimes hysterical. Barbara Boyd, in a text entitled, 'Carl Schmitt: Dick Cheney's Eminence Grise,' *Executive Intelligence Review*, 6 January 2006, thus presents Carl Schmitt as the theoretician of the 'absolute enemy' and the author of books whose promotion was organised 'by the synarchist banking crowd.' She affirms that 'the close relationship between Carl Schmitt and Leo Strauss [...] suggests that Dick Cheney's advocacy of the *Führerprinzip* is not a matter of coincidence' (sic), and that 'Schmitt's works proved useful in the 1970s' dirty work of George Shultz and Henry Kissinger in overthrowing the Allende government in Chile.' In another text, published some months earlier ('Leo Strauss y Carl Schmitt, el jurista de Hitler,' *EIR — Resumen ejecutivo*, March 2005), she affirmed very seriously that the works of Schmitt were 'in great part financed at the international level by the Straussians of the Lynde and Harry Bradley Foundation.' Qualifying Schmitt at the same time as the 'intellectual godfather of Strauss' and the 'Hannibal Lecter of modern politics' (sic), she went so far as to present Alexandre Kojève as an 'ideologue of universal fascism.' The first text of Barbara Boyd has been reprinted in a brochure published in January 2006 (for the purpose of contesting the nomination of Samuel Alito to the Supreme Court): *Cheney's 'Schmittlerian' Drive for Dictatorship: Children of Satan IV* (Leesburg: Lyndon LaRouche PAC, 2006). In his *Executive Intelligence Review*, Lyndon B. LaRouche himself declares that Dick Cheney and Paul Wolfowitz are 'fascists,' that 'Strauss and Kojève have openly defended the same fascist philosophy as that of Carl Schmitt, the master of the thought of Strauss,' and so on.

New School for Social Research, Alan Wolfe, 'A Fascist Philosopher Helps Us Understand Contemporary Politics,' which appeared in 2004 in *The Chronicle of Higher Education*. Wolfe writes that in order to understand the contemporary politics of the Republican Party, one should know not only Leo Strauss, but Carl Schmitt. The article emphasises the surprising interest that numerous authors classified as Left-wing have in Schmittian thought. It then asserts that, in the United States, 'Conservatives have absorbed Schmitt's conception of politics much more thoroughly than liberals' and claims that Schmitt's way of thinking about politics pervades the contemporary *zeitgeist* in which Republican conservatism has flourished.[9]

Making, in her turn, allusion to the commentaries on Carl Schmitt's book *The Concept of the Political*, that Leo Strauss published at the beginning of the thirties, Anne Norton writes, 'Strauss gave *The Concept of the Political* a more than sympathetic reading. Strauss, Schmitt believed, had understood him better than any other man, better, perhaps, than he understood himself. He had incorporated Strauss' understanding into his work. Strauss was to incorporate elements of Schmitt's work in his own critique of liberalism.'[10] Shadia B. Drury also presents Leo Strauss as someone who 'radicalised' (sic) the theses of Schmitt.[11] Sébastien Fath, too, speaking of Leo Strauss, refers to 'his professor and collaborator Carl Schmitt.'[12] Stanford V. Levinson, professor at the University of Texas, claims that Carl Schmitt is the true inspirer of the politics of the Bush administration.[13] One could cite many other examples.

Each of these statements, which make one think that Schmitt and Strauss fundamentally thought the same thing and that Schmitt is today the 'secret master' of the White House, is more surprising and false than the next. They emanate from authors who often have only a

---

9 *The Chronicle of Higher Education*, 2 April 2004.

10 *Leo Strauss and the Politics of American Empire*, op. cit., p. 40. For a critique of Anne Norton's book, cf. Peter Berkowitz, *New York Post Online Edition*, 3 October 2004. Like many other authors, Berkowitz has pointed out numerous factual errors in this book. He also emphasises its superficial character and the inability of the author to prove what she proposes.

11 *Leo Strauss and the American Right*, op. cit., pp. 65-97 ('Strauss's German Connection: Schmitt and Heidegger').

12 *Dieu bénisse l'Amérique: La religion de la Maison-Blanche* (Paris: Seuil, 2004), p. 206.

13 *Daedalus*, Summer 2004.

very superficial knowledge of Strauss' thought, and apparently know nothing of Schmitt's.[14] First of all, nothing indicates that the work of Schmitt was ever truly read in American neoconservative circles.[15] Besides, Alan Wolfe and others make a quite typical misinterpretation which has several consequences: Carl Schmitt having all his life severely criticised liberalism, they think that the neoconservatives adopted his critiques of liberalism. This is to forget that the term 'liberalism' has a totally different, if not opposite, meaning in Europe than

14 Sébastien Fath writes, here not without reason, that 'President Bush, Jr., himself has probably not read a line of Strauss' (op. cit., p. 219). One can, without great risk of being wrong, think that he has never read a single line of Carl Schmitt either. Peter Sirk remarks for his part that it would be erroneous to presume 'that everyone who deploys arguments analogous to those of Schmitt do so because they have been directly influenced by Schmitt, or even indirectly influenced by some complicated, conspiratorial or subterranean route' (*Carl Schmitt, Crown Jurist of the Third Reich: On Preemptive War, Military Occupation, and World Empire* [Lewiston: Edwin Mellen Press, 2005]), p. 35. Chantal Mouffe comes to identical conclusions in *On the Political* (Abingdon: Routledge, 2005), pp. 77-80. Cf. also Linda S. Bishai and Andreas Behnke, 'War, Violence, and the Displacement of the Political', in Louiza Odysseos and Fabio Petito (eds.), *The International Political Thought of Carl Schmitt: Terror, Liberal War and the Crisis of Global Order* (London: Routledge, 2007), pp. 107-123; and James O'Connor, *Exceptions, Distinctions, and Processes of Identification: The 'Concrete Thought' of Carl Schmitt and US Neoconservatism as Seen through Readings of Kenneth Burke and Jacques Derrida*, Master's thesis (Helsinki: University of Helsinki, 2006).

15 It is only recently that the principal works of Carl Schmitt have been translated into English. Let us cite, in the order of publication: *The Concept of the Political: Expanded Edition* (Chicago: University of Chicago Press, 2007); *Political Theology: Four Chapters on the Concept of Sovereignty* (Cambridge: MIT Press, 1985); *The Crisis of Parliamentary Democracy* (Cambridge: MIT Press, 1985); *Political Romanticism* (Cambridge: MIT Press, 1986); 'The Plight of European Jurisprudence,' *Telos* 83, (Spring 1990): pp. 35-70; *The Leviathan in the State of Thomas Hobbes: Meaning and Failure of a Political Symbol*, (Westport: Greenwood Press, 1996); *Roman Catholicism and Political Form* (Westport: Greenwood Press, 1996); *The Tyranny of Values* (Washington: Plutarch Press, 1996); *Land and Sea*, (Washington: Plutarch Press, 1997); *State, Movement, People: The Triadic Structure of the Political Unity* (Corvallis: Plutarch Press, 2001); *The 'Nomos' of the Earth in the International Law of the 'Jus Publicum Europaeum'* (New York: Telos Press, 2003); *Legality and Legitimacy* (Durham: Duke University Press, 2004); *On the Three Types of Juristic Thought* (Westport: Praeger, 2004); *Theory of the Partisan: Intermediate Commentary on the Concept of the Political*, (New York: Telos Press, 2007) (another translation: 'The Theory of the Partisan: A Commentary/Remark on the Concept of the Political,' *The New Centennial Review* IV [2004], 3); and *War / Non-war? A Dilemma* (Corvallis: Plutarch Press, 2005). One notes, besides, that a certain number of Anglo-Saxon 'Schmittians' are situated politically on the Left, as is shown by the articles that appeared in the New York journal *Telos* (founded in the sixties by the American disciples of Theodor W. Adorno and Max Horkheimer, leaders of the Frankfurt School) or the works of Joseph W. Bendersky, Ellen Kennedy, Gary L. Ulmen, Chantal Mouffe Gopal Balakrishnan, and others.

in the United States. What the Europeans call 'liberalism' is in fact much closer to what one in America classifies as 'conservatism' than to what one there understands by the term 'liberalism.' For Schmitt, as for the majority of continental European authors, 'conservatism' implies a predisposition in favour of the state and a pessimistic conception of human nature, whereas 'liberalism' is defined by belief in progress, adherence to the ideology of human rights, confidence in the system of free trade, faith in the superiority of the market, an individualistic approach to society, and so on (all things criticised by Carl Schmitt). From the European point of view, the great liberal theoreticians are John Locke and Adam Smith, the most liberal contemporary politicians Ronald Reagan, Margaret Thatcher or... George W. Bush. In other words, in Europe, 'liberal' is directly opposed to 'social,' whereas in the United States the 'liberals' are, on the contrary, those who are favourable to social interventions of the state. Consequently, when Alan Wolfe writes, for example, '[T]he most important lesson Schmitt teaches is that the differences between liberals and conservatives are not just over the policies they advocate but also over the meaning of politics itself,' and then adds, 'Liberals think of politics as a means; conservatives as an end,'[16] he gratuitously leads the reader astray (and proves at the same time that he himself has not understood anything of what Schmitt says). Anne Norton commits the same mistake when she writes, 'Leo Strauss joined Carl Schmitt and Alexandre Kojève in their critique of liberalism and liberal institutions,'[17] thus making it appear that these authors attack an ideology that the Americans situate on the Left of the political landscape, whereas in Europe it is situated on the Right. The very correct observation of Francis Fukuyama, according to which 'the [American] neoconservatives do not in any way wish to defend the order of things as founded on hierarchy, tradition and a pessimistic view of human nature,'[18] suffices to show how much separates this tendency from the thought of Carl Schmitt, who, on the contrary, explicitly makes a 'pessimistic' conception of human nature one of the cornerstones of his system.

Schmitt is in fact so little 'conservative' in the American sense of the term that he places the notion of private property at the centre

---

16 Alan Wolfe, 'A Fascist Philosopher Helps Us Understand Contemporary Politics.'
17 Anne Norton, *Leo Strauss and the Politics of American Empire*, p. 109.
18 *The Wall Street Journal*, 24 December 2002.

of the 'moral-economic polarity' which he denounces strongly as most alien to the essence of politics. The 'liberal concepts,' he writes, 'typically move between ethics (intellectuality) and economics (trade). From this polarity they attempt to annihilate the political [...]. The concept of private law serves as a lever and the notion of private property forms the center of the globe, whose poles — ethics and economics — are only its contrasting eminations.'[19] The most charitable conclusion is thus, once again, that Anne Norton herself has never read a line of Carl Schmitt.[20]

What, really, were the relations between Leo Strauss and Carl Schmitt? The dossier is thin, and the link between the two men rather tenuous. It occurs, besides, within a very short period of time. Strauss was, in 1932, one of the first to write a commentary on the second edition of Schmitt's book on the concept of the political.[21] His commentary was by no means an unconditional approval. It was, on the contrary, a critical appreciation, even if the critique was expressed in a very polite manner. In his comments,[22] Strauss reproaches Schmitt

---

19 *The Concept of the Political*, p. 71.

20 One notices it also on p. 153, where it makes of Schmitt a sort of apologist for warlike values (or of the martial conception of life), which is the exact opposite of his thought. 'War,' she writes, 'seemed to Carl Schmitt, and still seems to some of the students of Leo Strauss, to be the activity which would restore seriousness to life. [...] War would restore virtue as well. Without war, heroism and courage, valor and sacrifice are lost,' etc. The reality is exactly the opposite. Schmitt totally rejects, for example, the views of the young Ernst Jünger, his 'agonal' conception of existence, and his partially aesthetic perception of war. War, in the eyes of Schmitt, has no intrinsic value. It is only a means of reaching a political goal or of reestablishing peace.

21 *Der Begriff des Politischen: Mit einer Rede über das Zeitalter der Neutralisierung und Entpolitisierung* (Munich-Leipzig: Duncker & Humblot, 1932). This is a revised edition. The first edition dates from 1928 and was itself preceded by a first version following the text of a speech made in Berlin on 10 May 1927 (*Archiv für Sozialwissenschaft und Sozialpolitik*, LVIII, 1, [September 1927]: pp. 1-33).

22 Leo Strauss, 'Anmerkungen zu Carl Schmitt, "Der Begriff des Politischen" (1932),' in *Archiv für Sozialwissenschaft und Sozialpolitik* LXVII, 6, (August-September 1932), pp. 732-749; text reprinted in Leo Strauss, *Hobbes' politische Wissenschaft* (Neuwied: Luchterhand, 1965), pp. 161-181, latest edition: in *Hobbes' politische Wissenschaft und zugehörige Schriften — Briefe*, volume 3 of *Gesammelte Schriften* (Stuttgart-Weimar: J.B. Metzler, 2001), pp. 217-242, as well as in Heinrich Meier's book (cf. note 23). The English text, 'Comments on Carl Schmitt's *Der Begriff des Politischen*,' has been reprinted in Leo Strauss, *Spinoza's Critique of Religion* (New York: Schocken Books, 1965), pp. 331-351, then in Leo Strauss, *An Introduction to Political Philosophy* (Detroit: Wayne State University Press, 1989). One will note that Strauss presents a reading of Schmitt's book that is very different from that prepared at the same time by Hans Morgenthau in his thesis on international law,

of remaining 'within the horizon of liberalism' even while claiming to make a radical critique of it, and of not having understood that Hobbes — who is in his eyes the *antipolitical* thinker par excellence — is none other than the one 'who had laid the foundations of liberalism,' by virtue notably of the individualistic premises of his doctrine. He also states that the true foundation of the position of Schmitt vis-à-vis liberalism is his Catholicism. These remarks led Carl Schmitt to modify certain passages of his book.[23] In the final edition, Schmitt recognises that he was led to reformulate certain of his concepts and to correct himself following the critiques formulated by Leo Strauss, whom he describes merely as an 'attentive reader' of his work.[24]

Also in 1932, Carl Schmitt wrote a letter recommending Leo Strauss for a fellowship at the Rockefeller Foundation, a fellowship which allowed the latter to pursue his studies in France and England before he emigrated definitively to the United States in 1937 (where he

---

La notion du politique et la théorie des différends internationaux (Geneva: Librairie du recueil Sirey, 1933). On this point, cf. Hans-Karl Pichler, 'The Weberian Legacy, The Godfathers of "Truth": Max Weber and Carl Schmitt in Morgenthau's Theory of Power Politics,' *Review of International Studies* XXIV, 2 (April 1998), pp. 185-200; and Martti Koskenniemi, 'Carl Schmitt, Hans Morgenthau, and the Image of Law in International Relations,' in Michael Byers (ed.), *The Role of Law in International Politics: Essays on International Relations and International Law* (Oxford: Oxford University Press, 2000), pp. 17-34 (text reprinted and elaborated under the title 'Out of Europe: Carl Schmitt, Hans Morgenthau, and the Turn to "International Relations" in Martti Koskenniemi, *The Gentle Civilizer of Nations: The Rise and Fall of International Law 1870-1960* [Cambridge: Cambridge University Press, 2001], pp. 413-509).

23 *Der Begriff der Politischen* went through a third edition in 1933. The version of 1932 was republished in 1963, with a Foreword and three complementary 'corollaries.' It is this version which has since been constantly reedited (the thirteenth edition being published in 2002). The different versions of the work, as well as the text of Strauss, have been the object of an exhaustive study by Heinrich Meier (*Carl Schmitt, Leo Strauss und der 'Begriff des Politischen': Zu einem Dialog unter Abwesenden — Mit Leo Strauss Aufsatz über den 'Begriff des Politischen' und drei unveröffentlichten Briefen an Carl Schmitts aus den Jahren 1932-33* (Stuttgart: J.B. Metzler, 1988), p. 141; English translation: *Carl Schmitt and Leo Strauss: The Hidden Dialogue, Including Strauss's Notes on Schmitt's 'Concept of the Political' and Three Letters from Strauss to Schmitt* (Chicago: University of Chicago Press, 1995). Apart from the text of Leo Strauss, the work includes three unpublished letters addressed to Carl Schmitt in 1932-33. In France, in addition to the version appearing in Heinrich Meier's book, the text of Strauss has also been translated by Jean-Louis Schlegel as an annex to Carl Schmitt's book *Parlementarisme et démocratie* (Paris: Seuil 1988), pp. 187-214.

24 *La notion de politique* (Paris: Flammarion, 1992), pp. 183 and 186.

taught political philosophy at the University of Chicago from 1949). Heinrich Meier has published the text of the three letters addressed to Carl Schmitt by Leo Strauss between 13 March 1932 and 10 July 1933. In the first of these letters, Strauss thanks Carl Schmitt for the help that he has given him and confines himself to politely expressing to him his respect for his work, which is indeed the least he could do *vis-à-vis* someone to whom he was indebted. In the second letter, dated 4 September 1932, he specifies the critiques expressed in his article. In the third, he asks Schmitt about a project of a critical edition of the work of Hobbes in which he says he wishes to participate. This project never materialised. Schmitt never replied to the last of these letters, and we do not have the text of his replies to the other two, supposing that there were any. No other correspondence between the two men is known, even though it is possible that Strauss wrote once more to Schmitt in 1934. The relations between Leo Strauss and Carl Schmitt did not go very far. Carl Schmitt — who, in 1932-33, could at that time know only the first part of Strauss' work on Hobbes, as well as his critique of Spinoza which appeared in 1931 — would confine himself to citing his name in his book on the *Leviathan* which appeared in 1938.[25] As for Strauss, he would never publish anything more on Carl Schmitt.[26]

---

25 *The Leviathan in the State Theory of Thomas Hobbes: Meaning and Failure of a Political Symbol* (Westport, CT: Greenwood Press, 1996).

26 On the relations between Schmitt and Strauss, cf. Paul Gottfried, 'Schmitt and Strauss,' in *Telos* 96, (Summer 1993), pp. 167-176; John P. McCormick, 'Fear, Technology, and the State: Carl Schmitt, Leo Strauss and the Revival of Hobbes in Weimar and National Socialist Germany,' in *Political Theory* XXII, 2 (1994), pp. 619-652; Robert Howse, 'From Legitimacy to Dictatorship — and Back Again: Leo Strauss's Critique of the Anti-Liberalism of Carl Schmitt,' in David Dyzenhaus (ed.), *Carl Schmitt's Challenge to Liberalism*, special issue of *The Canadian Journal of Law and Jurisprudence*, X, 1 (January 1997), pp. 77-104, text reprinted in David Dyzenhaus (ed.), *Law as Politics: Carl Schmitt's Critique of Liberalism* (Durham: Duke University Press, 1998), pp. 56-90 ; and 'The Use and Abuse of Leo Strauss in the Schmitt Revival on the German Right — The Case of Heinrich Meier' (unpublished text) ; Eduardo Hernando Nieto, '¿Teología política o filosofía política? La amistosa conversación entre Carl Schmitt y Leo Strauss,' in Jorge E. Dotti and Julio Pinto (ed.), *Carl Schmitt: Su época y su pensamiento* (Buenos Aires: Eudeba, 2002), pp. 189-209; Claudia Hilb, 'Más allá del liberalism: Notas sobre las "Anmerkungen" de Leo Strauss al "Concepto de lo politico" de Carl Schmitt,' ibid., pp. 211-227; Miguel E. Vatter, 'Strauss and Schmitt as Readers of Hobbes and Spinoza: On the Relation between Political Theology and Liberalism,' in *CR: The New Centennial Review* IV, 3 (Winter 2004), pp. 161-214; Carlo Altini, *La storia della filosofia come filosofia politica. Carl Schmitt et Leo Strauss lettori di Thomas Hobbes* (Pisa: ETS, 2004); D. Janssens, 'A Change of Orientation: Leo Strauss's "Comments" on Carl Schmitt

We shall not investigate the contents of the political philosophy of Leo Strauss here. Let us say only that it is sufficient to read Strauss' work to confirm that his inspiration is radically different from that of Carl Schmitt. Heinrich Meier is one of those who have best shown the radical incompatibility ('insuperable opposition') existing between the political *theology* of Schmitt and the political *philosophy* of Strauss: '*inter auctoritatem et philosophiam nihil est medium.*' 'The gulf between political theology and political philosophy is insuperable,' he writes, 'dividing Carl Schmitt and Leo Strauss even where both seem to agree in their political positions or in fact agree in their political critique of a common opponent.'[27] 'Whereas the political does have central significance for the thought of Leo Strauss, the

Revisited,' *Interpretation* XXXIII, 1, (2005), pp. 93-104; Reinhard Mehring, 'Carl Schmitt, Leo Strauss, Thomas Hobbes und die Philosophie,' in *Philosophisches Jahrbuch* CXII, 2 (2005), pp. 380-394; Walter Schmidt, 'Politische Theologie III. Anmerkungen zu Carl Schmitt und Leo Strauss,' in Charlotte Gaitanides (ed.), *Europa und seine Verfassung: Festschrift für Manfred Zuleeg zum siebzigsten Geburtstag* (Baden-Baden: Nomos, 2005), pp. 15-34; and Jianhong Chen, *Between Politics and Philosophy: A Study of Leo Strauss in Dialogue with Carl Schmitt*, doctoral thesis (Louvain-la-Neuve: Université catholique de Louvain, 2006). Cf. also John Gunnell, 'Strauss before Straussianism: The Weimar Conversation,' in *Review of Politics* LII, 1 (Winter 1990). In an interview published by the daily *La Repubblica* ('Il filosofo e la politica,' 24 March 2005), Altini also recalls that Strauss accused Schmitt of 'lacking in coherence' in his critique of liberalism and, besides, of 'proposing an ideological reading of Hobbes.' He specifies in this regard that 'Strauss never thought that the prince needed a philosophical adviser.' Paul Gottfried writes, 'In short, there is nothing in the written record of Strauss' relation to Schmitt to indicate his future role in founding a school whose adherents today have become global missionaries for American "liberal democracy"' ('Schmitt and Strauss,' p. 173). A Master's seminar led by professors Heinz Dieter Kittsteiner and Michael Minkenberg took place, besides, between 14 April and 14 July 2005, at the Europa-Universität Viadrina Frankfurt/Oder, on the subject 'Carl Schmitt, Leo Strauss und die amerikanischen Neokonservativen.' Cf. also Michael Zank, 'Beyond the "Theological-Political Predicament": Toward a Contextualization of the Early Strauss,' Boston University, 2005.

27 *Carl Schmitt and Leo Strauss: The Hidden Dialogue*, p. 43. Cf. also Benjamin Sax, 'The Distinction between Political Theology and Political Philosophy,' in *The European Legacy*, August 2002, pp. 499-502. By Heinrich Meier, who is also the publishing director of the complete works of Leo Strauss in Germany, one will also read *Die Denkbewegung von Leo Strauss. Die Geschichte der Philosophie und die Intention des Philosophes* (Stuttgart-Weimar: J.B. Metzler, 1996) (Eng. tr.: *The Theological-Political Problem: On the Theme of Leo Strauss* [Cambridge: Cambridge University Press, 2005]), and *Das theologisch-politische Problem: Zum Thema Leo Strauss* (Stuttgart: J.B. Metzler, 2003) (Eng. Tr.: *Leo Strauss and the Theological-Political Problem* [Cambridge: Cambridge University Press, 2006]). On Leo Strauss, cf. also Daniel Tanguay, *Leo Strauss: Une biographie intellectuelle* (Paris: Grasset, 2003); and Park Sung-rae, *Leo Strauss* (Seoul: Gimm-Young, 2005).

enemy and enmity do not,' he further states, which clearly shows the error of the interpretations attributing to Strauss a thought governed by the idea of hostility.[28] There is therefore, to repeat the expression of Heinrich Meier, a 'gulf' between the two men. The authors who today claim to see in Leo Strauss the successor and disciple of Schmittian thought cannot be taken seriously.

The hypothesis that Carl Schmitt influenced the American neo-conservatives through the intermediary of Leo Strauss is only a fable. But Carl Schmitt's thought is, on the other hand, as numerous observers have noted, still topical, in particular since the attacks of 11 September 2001 — a topicality which international developments, as well as certain initiatives by the American government, have continued to nourish in recent years. In this essay we shall examine the main reasons why Carl Schmitt remains topical today.

---

28 *Carl Schmitt and Leo Strauss*, p. 87. Carole Widmaier also emphasises that 'Leo Strauss is not Carl Schmitt: the friend/enemy antagonism is not [for Strauss] what defines the political relationship' ('Leo Strauss est-il néoconservateur? L'épreuve des textes,' p. 35).

1. From 'Regulated War' to the Return of the 'Just War'

'**S**tatesmen should, above all, have the ability to distinguish friends from enemies,' writes Irving Kristol, one of the principal American neoconservatives in the journal of his son William, *The Weekly Standard*.[29] Carl Schmitt would not have disagreed with this statement; neither in its descriptive aspect nor in its normative aspect. The very essence of politics consists, according to him, not so much in the fact of hostility as in the possibility of making a distinction between public friends and public enemies — not when a conflict has already materialised, but in respect of potential conflicts. Politics, in other words, implies conflict: a strictly pacific vision of social life is an *unpolitical* vision. Consequently, the uncertainty of the identity of the enemy constitutes one of the greatest dangers in politics.

Schmitt, however, does not maintain the famous formula of Clausewitz, according to whom war is only the continuation of politics by other means. On the contrary, he emphasises that 'its meaning for the understanding of the essence of politics is thereby still not exhausted.'[30] War is itself, just like the state of emergency of which we shall speak again below, a border concept (*Grenzbegriff*). It is incontestably an extension of politics because politics implies hostility, but it cannot be reduced to this because it has its own essence. Schmitt emphasises that war has its own perspective and its own rules, and that the latter 'all presuppose that the political decision has already been made as to who the enemy is.'[31] In supporting the view that politics, even in peacetime, possesses a conflictual dimension, Schmitt adopts a position close to that of Clausewitz, but which should not be confused with it; it tends rather to complete it and to go beyond it.

---

29 'The Neoconservative Persuasion,' in *The Weekly Standard*, 25 August 2003.

30 *The Concept of the Political*, p. 34. Cf. also Carl Schmitt, 'Clausewitz als politischer Denker: Bemerkungen und Hinweise,' in *Der Staat* VI, 4 (1967): pp. 479-502.

31 *The Concept of the Political*, p. 34.

Clausewitz sees what is political in war, Schmitt what is conflictual in politics.

Schmitt posits at the same time a political conception of hostility. The enemy must, according to him, be regarded politically: he must remain a *political* enemy, that is, an adversary that one must fight, certainly, but with whom one can one day make peace. In the perspective of the *jus publicum europaeum*,[32] peace clearly remains the aim of war: every war is naturally concluded by a peace treaty. And, as it is only with an enemy that one can make peace, that implies that the belligerents *mutually recognise one other*. Such a recognition (of the Other, both in his similarities and in his differences) is the very condition that makes peace possible, for only a belligerent whom one has previously recognised can be invited to conclude a peace treaty. This is why Schmitt affirms that an absolute war, a total war, would be a disaster from a strictly political point of view since, by attempting to annihilate the enemy, it eliminates the element which constitutes politics.[33]

Of the 'regulated war,' characteristic of the Westphalian order founded on the *jus publicum europaeum* which replaced the old *respublica christiana*,[34] Carl Schmitt says that it is a war where the belligerents 'respect each other at war as enemies and do not treat one another as criminals, so that a peace treaty becomes possible and even remains the normal, mutually accepted end of war.'[35] War conducted according to the old law of nations follows rules governing, for example, the conduct of troops towards prisoners and civilians, the respect for neutral parties, the immunity of ambassadors, the rules of surrendering a stronghold, and the modalities of concluding a peace treaty. It almost never aims at overthrowing a sovereign or changing the government of a country, and is usually fought simply to achieve territorial objectives. Finally, it is an exclusively inter-state reality. The

---

32 Schmitt used this term in his book, *The Nomos of the Earth*, to designate the reorganisation of the world and the first attempts at international law made by the European colonial powers during a period which he defined as beginning in the fifteenth century and drawing to a close at the end of the First World War.-Ed.

33 Cf. Mika Ojakangas, *A Philosophy of Concrete Life: Carl Schmitt and the Political Thought of Late Modernity* (Jyväskylä: SoPhi, 2004), pp. 71-72.

34 In Medieval times this term designated the Christian world.-Ed.

35 *The Theory of the Partisan: A Commentary/Remark on the Concept of the Political*, translated by A. C. Goodson (Lansing: Michigan State University, 2004), p. 6. Available at obinfonet.ro/docs/tpnt/tpntres/cschmitt-theory-of-the-partisan.pdf.

state enjoys at the same time a monopoly of legitimate violence (Max Weber) and a monopoly of political decision (Schmitt), meaning that private wars and family vendettas are forbidden (a prohibition that was gradually extended to the duel). This means that individuals can only be public enemies as members or citizens of a state, and not individually in themselves. In the Westphalian order each sovereign's *jus ad bellum*[36] is recognised, for it is part of the liberties or rights constitutive of state sovereignty. Such a system excludes the very idea of 'international police.' It also recognises the legitimacy of the neutrality of third parties.

In the eyes of Schmitt, the great merit of the *jus publicum europaeum* has been to substitute for the Medieval doctrine of the 'just war,' with its moral origin, a political doctrine of the 'war within protocols' or 'war in due form' (Vattel).[37] This new doctrine was introduced when the sovereign states asserted themselves, notably in relation to the Roman Church (as a result of the 'neutralisation' of the religious wars that had divided and devastated Europe). This development led first to the recognition of the sovereign character, and equal sovereignty, of states, then to the emphasis no longer of *jus ad bellum* (the rules governing when a war can be lawfully started) but of *jus in bello* (the rules governing how a war, once begun, should be conducted). From then on, it is no longer the war that is accepted when it is declared 'just,' but the enemy who becomes 'just' insofar as he is recognised. War between states is thus a fundamentally symmetrical war. It is modelled on the duel, in which the adversaries mutually recognise each other's equality and both observe the rules of the same code. Thanks to the formal concept of the *justus hostis*,[38] of the recognised enemy, international law makes war a regulated confrontation between sovereign states that are formally equal, basically amounting to 'a duel between cavaliers seeking satisfaction.'[39]

Far from thinking that war suspends the rule of law, Schmitt pleads relentlessly that, on the contrary, war should always be subjected to

---

36 Latin: 'right to war,' meaning the circumstances that must arise before a nation can go to war.-Ed.

37 Emerich de Vattel (1714-1767) was the Swiss philosopher who wrote *The Law of Nations*, which is regarded as one of the foundational texts of modern international law.-Ed.

38 A key concept for Schmitt, referring to a 'just enemy.'-Ed.

39 Schmitt, *The Theory of the Partisan*, p. 36.

the principles of the *jus in bello*. As Norbert Campagna writes, 'The Schmittian concept of war is a profoundly juridical concept.'[40] The *jus publicum europaeum*, in instituting uncrossable boundaries, has prevented armed conflicts from degenerating into total war, that is, into 'blind and reciprocal extermination.' It is in this way, writes Schmitt, that we have succeeded in 'rationalising, humanisation, juridifying, in short: circumscribing war,'[41] i.e., limiting it. The doctrine of the 'war in due form' is equivalent to a limitation of war, for it makes the war of annihilation impossible. The *jus publicum europaeum* has been the *katechon*[42] par excellence, the great delayer of the return of 'just wars' within the horizon of juridical universalism. War is thus for Schmitt never an end in itself. For him it does not even have a value in the sense of a symbolic (or aesthetic) representation of human existence: 'warlike values,' as already noted, are totally alien to him. Such a conception of war, even while recognising that war is inevitable, is clearly in the service of peace. Even when politics is defined by the element of conflictuality that it contains, war is posited as an exception, as a temporary disturbance of the normal order of things that is peace.

Total war is a war which, in contrast to the regulated war, does not recognise any limitations. It is the type of war which is exalted in biblical monotheism, under the form of the 'obligatory holy war' (*milhemit mitzva*) conducted against the enemies of God. The enemy is then no longer a simple adversary with whom one can be reconciled, but a figure of evil who must be eradicated. The Book of Joshua, notably, describes at great length the extermination of the enemy, the destruction of his towns, the murder of women, children and even animals, the mutilation of the corpses, and so on — all things presented as a sacred duty.[43]

It is from a re-elaboration of this biblical doctrine by Christian theologians that the doctrine of the just war (*bellum justum*) was born in the Middle Ages, which is no longer a war explicitly willed by God,

---

40 *Le droit, la politique et la guerre: Deux chapitres sur la doctrine de Carl Schmitt* (Québec: Presses de l'Université Laval, 2004), p. 12.

41 *The Nomos of the Earth*, p. 121.

42 In traditional Christian doctrine, this is something that prevents the Antichrist from appearing.-Ed.

43 Cf. D. J. Bederman, *International Law in Antiquity* (Cambridge: Cambridge University Press, 2001); and Danilo Zolo, 'Una "guerra globale" monoteistica,' in *Iride* 2 (2003), pp. 223-240 (reprinted in *Trasgressioni*, 42, January-April 2006, pp. 17-33).

but a war which can be conducted legitimately provided that it obeys certain rules and conditions.[44] The classical conditions of the just war are the just cause, the legitimate defence, the proportionality of means, and the last resort. War must be conducted by a legitimate authority, have peace as its aim, respond to a 'just intention,' and obey certain rules in the conduct of the operations, such as avoiding unnecessary bloodshed. As Danilo Zolo stresses, it is also an essentially worldly war and which supposes the presence of a stable *auctoritas spiritualis*,[45] in this case that of the Roman Catholic Church. An important point is that these rules are valid only for the people of the *respublica christiana*, and do not apply to pagans, 'infidels,' 'barbarians,' 'savages,' pirates and so on, who can never hope to benefit from them. As a result, all the crusades are *ipso facto* just wars and pontifical mandates valid for the territorial conquest of lands belonging to non-Christian peoples. Unrestricted enmity has thus been banished from the European world. The theory of the just war introduces a discriminatory conception of war: if there are just wars, there are also unjust wars. But it also divides humanity into two categories: against the 'infidels' and the 'barbarians' everything is permitted.

Carl Schmitt, in his essay of 1938 on 'the turn towards the discriminatory conception of war,'[46] situates the beginning of the collapse of the old law of nations around 1890. The process would be completed during the First World War, which begins under traditional forms but turns, from 1917, into a war of a new type. The era of the 'modern just war' begins with the signature of the Treaty of Versailles and the will of the Allies to bring Kaiser Wilhelm II to justice, for 'supreme

---

44 Cf. Yves Leroy de la Brière, *Le droit de juste guerre: Tradition théologique et adaptations contemporaines* (Paris: Pedone, 1938); Frederick H. Russell, *The Just War in the Middle Ages* (Cambridge: Cambridge University Press, 1975); J. T. Johnson, *Just War Tradition and the Restraint of War* (Princeton: Princeton University Press, 1981); William Vincent O'Brien, *The Conduct of Just and Limited War* (New York: Praeger, 1981); Jean Bethke Elshtain (ed.), *Just War Theory* (Oxford: Basil Blackwell, 1991); United States Military Academy (ed.), *Just War Reader* (Stanford: Thomson Custom, 2004); and Jean-Philippe Schreiber (ed.), *Théologies de la guerre* (Brussels: Editions de l'Université de Bruxelles, 2006).

45 Latin: 'spiritual authority.'-Ed.

46 *Die Wendung zum diskriminierenden Kriegsbegriff* (Munich-Leipzig: Duncker & Humblot, 1938) (text reprinted in Carl Schmitt, *Frieden oder Pazifismus? Arbeiten zum Völkerrecht und zur Internationalen Politik 1924-1978*, ed. Günter Maschke [Berlin: Duncker & Humblot, 2005], pp. 518-597). English version: 'The Turn to the Discriminating Concept of War,' in Carl Schmitt, *Writings on War* (Cambridge: Polity Press, 2011).

outrage against international morality and against the sanctity of treaties,' that is, for having started the war. In this way one of the founding principles of the *jus publicum europaeum* was abandoned, according to which there cannot be any power on Earth which has the right to judge the sovereign of a nation (Hobbes: *Non est potestas super terram quae comparetur ei*).[47] Henceforth, one who declares war can be regarded as a criminal who should be brought to justice and punished. The consequences will prove disastrous. 'What Schmitt considers,' writes Norbert Campagna, '[...] is that wars are apparently no longer battles between adversaries who recognise one anothers' rights and status, but tend more and more to become police actions opposing the police of the international order to the state judged an aggressor. War becomes thus a kind of battle between the forces of good and the forces of evil, between those who arrogate to themselves the right to judge and those who should be put on the dock.'[48]

Is the just war of the modern age a military or a political concept? It far exceeds the demands of a simple armed fight, but it also implies a representation of the enemy that goes beyond Carl Schmitt's properly political definition of the term. Just war is in fact a moral concept, where evil is posited as an absolute. By the same token, it is equally antipolitical in that it seeks to annihilate the enemy, who is the defining element of politics. The 'discriminatory' modern war, Schmitt would say, 'also is a retreat from the juridical concept of the enemy.'[49] The ideological appropriation of the concept of war and of the principle of recognition (or non-recognition) invariably leads to making a criminal or an outlaw of the enemy. 'The present theory of just war,' writes Schmitt, 'aims to distinguish the opponent who wages unjust war. War becomes an "offense" in the criminal sense, and the aggressor becomes a "felon" in the most extreme criminal sense: an outlaw, a pirate.'[50]

To say that the enemy is a criminal is a way of denying him all political claims, thus disqualifying him politically. The criminal cannot claim an opinion or an idea whose degree of truth or falsehood it

---

47 From Job 41:24, meaning 'there is no power on earth to be compared to him,' referring to the monstrous leviathan. Hobbes placed the quote beneath the cover illustration on his book of the same name.-Ed.

48 *Le droit, la politique et la guerre*, p. 99.

49 *The Nomos of the Earth*, p. 124.

50 *The Nomos of the Earth*, p. 122.

may be necessary to evaluate; he is an intrinsically destructive being. When one fights in the name of what is absolutely valuable, the enemy is absolutely devalued: he is declared an absolute non-entity. The criminalisation of the enemy thus entails the effacement (*Hegungen*) of the limitations applied to war by European international law. 'The introduction (or reintroduction) of a moral perspective into the law,' writes Jean-François Kervégan, 'involves recourse to a new concept of the enemy, that of a total enemy, and ends in the transformation of the "limited" war, i.e., the classical war between juridically equal sovereign powers, into a total war.'[51] In fact, with the demonisation of the adversary, the annihilation of the enemy identified with absolute evil becomes more than a condition necessary for victory, it becomes a moral imperative. Carl Schmitt writes, 'Such a war is necessarily unusually intense and inhuman because, by transcending the limits of the political framework, it simultaneously degrades the enemy into moral and other categories and is forced to make of him a monster that must not only be defeated but also utterly destroyed.'[52]

The just war of modern times thus acquires at once a double character, that of a war eminently moral and that of a police operation destined to chastise an enemy perceived as a criminal. This evolution would reach its peak with the radical (provisional) disqualification of all warlike enterprises other than defensive ones, defining unilaterally declared wars of aggression as crimes.

The idea that one could definitively suppress war dates back at least to Erasmus, who affirmed in *Querela pacis* that 'there is no peace, even unjust, which is not preferable to the most just of wars.' Beginning in the second half of the eighteenth century, the idea spread that it was possible for humanity to move progressively towards what the Abbé de Saint-Pierre and Immanuel Kant called 'perpetual peace.' In the following century, this conviction took hold in very different milieus, but all equally heirs of the philosophy of the Enlightenment. The

---

51 'Carl Schmitt et "l'unité du monde"' in *Les Etudes philosophiques*, January 2004, pp. 11-12.

52 *The Concept of the Political*, p. 36. 'In a theological war,' comments Norbert Campagna, 'I wish to put an end to the existence of the other. In a political war, on the contrary, it is only a matter of putting an end to the risk posed by the other. In the first case, the other is the incarnation of evil, while in the second, he is only a risk that I should confront and against whom I should pit my strength' (*Le droit, la politique et la guerre*, p. 129).

liberals then thought that 'gentle commerce'[53] would progressively bring nations together, while the socialists imagined that the society of the future would abolish all causes of conflict, both sharing the same irenic and optimistic vision of 'progress.' Their hopes would be shattered by the events of the twentieth century, without, however, the pacifist illusion disappearing completely.

After the First World War, a persistent current continued to fight for the suppression and criminalisation of war. It is this mistaken position, and also the persistent ideal of a world where war has been eliminated forever, which leads today to the reappearance of the concept of the just war, and to the legitimation of war by a moral doctrine based on the ideology of human rights. This makes possible once again the war of annihilation, while technological progress permits the development of more powerful weapons than ever before. It is no longer a question of just war in the medieval sense, which still recognised certain limitations, but the just war conducted in the name of 'humanity,' of 'freedom' and of 'right.' Already, with the Kellogg-Briand Pact of 1928, it is not so much war in itself which was condemned as the right of nations and states to wage it. In this way, wars based on national interest were decreed to be unjust, whereas international war, war conducted in the name of humanity, became the new 'just war.' The danger of this development 'is that it [...] imposes on politics the mortal snare of a perpetual peace that has every likelihood of transforming itself into endless war.'[54] It is summarised in the formula, 'Perpetual war for perpetual peace.'

According to Carl Schmitt, 'The political world is a pluriverse, not a universe.'[55] The reason for this is that humanity is either a biological category or a moral category; it is not a political concept. Schmitt cites here the famous phrase of Proudhon: '[W]hoever invokes humanity wants to cheat.' 'When a state fights its political enemy in the name of humanity,' he explains, 'it is not a war for the sake of humanity, but a war wherein a particular state seeks to usurp a universal concept

---

53 'Gentle commerce,' championed by Montesquieu in *The Spirit of the Laws*, among other liberal thinkers, is a concept which holds that the encouragement of trade and other economic pursuits between nations reduces the likelihood of war.-Ed.

54 Etienne Balibar, 'Prolégomènes à la souveraineté: la frontière, l'Etat, le peuple,' in *Les Temps modernes*, November 2000, p. 55. Cf. also Günter Maschke, 'La décomposition du droit international,' interview published in *Krisis*, February 2005, pp. 43-66.

55 *The Concept of the Political*, p. 53.

against its military opponent.'[56] 'The concept of humanity,' he adds, 'is an ideological instrument especially useful to imperialist expansions. Humanity as such cannot wage war because it has no enemy, at least not on this planet. The concept of humanity excludes the concept of the enemy, because the enemy does not cease to be a human being — and hence there is no specific differentiation in that concept. [...] To confiscate the word humanity, to invoke and monopolise such a term probably has certain incalculable effects, such as denying the enemy the quality of being human and declaring him to be an outlaw of humanity; and a war can thereby be driven to the most extreme inhumanity.'[57]

In France, on 7 August 1793, the deputy Garnier de Saintes, had already proposed to the Convention[58] that the English statesman William Pitt should be declared 'the enemy of mankind,' in order that everybody might have the right to assassinate him. To fight in the name of humanity in fact means that one places oneself in the position of decreeing who is human and who is not. That is the paradox: all discussion that claims to efface the boundaries between men to extend the notion of 'us' to the totality of the human species ends in recreating in the midst of humanity itself a line of division and exclusion more radical than the ones preceding it. 'Only when man appeared to be the embodiment of absolute humanity did the other side of this concept appear in the form of a new enemy: the *inhuman*,' writes Schmitt.[59] War in the name of morality is thus the very model of the most inhumane warfare. Abstract universalism makes absolute enemies of its adversaries and transforms 'humanitarian' wars into wars of extermination.

Following the example of revolutionary France, the United States has never stopped proclaiming that the causes which it defends are consistent with the interests of humanity. '[The American] flag,' said Woodrow Wilson already, 'is the flag not only of America but of humanity.'[60] 'We are rapidly becoming a nation of humanitarian

56 *The Concept of the Political*, p. 54.

57 *The Concept of the Political*, p. 54.

58 Meaning the National Convention that was the legislative body of France during the French Revolution.

59 *The Nomos of the Earth*, p. 104.

60 Address of 4 July 1914, reproduced in Albert Bushnell Hart (ed.), *Selected Addresses and Public Papers of Woodrow Wilson* (Honolulu: University Press of the Pacific, 2002), p. 44.

crusaders,' noted Irving Babbitt in 1924.[61] 'This ideal of America is the hope of all mankind,' George W. Bush stated in a speech on 11 September 2002, one year after the attacks in New York and Washington.[62]

Instead of 'humanity,' Schmitt could just as well have spoken of 'freedom.' In the course of history, freedom has also been constantly cited by the United States to justify its enterprises of conquest or annexation. It was by the concept 'empire of freedom,' theorised by Jefferson, that it justified its first territorial conquests at the expense of Spain (in Cuba) and Mexico (in Texas). The intervention in Vietnam was also conducted in the name of 'freedom.' The same goes for the war on Iraq, which plunged that country into civil war and chaos. In his State of the Union Address of 28 January 2003, George W. Bush proclaimed, 'The liberty we prize is not America's gift to the world; it is God's gift to humanity.'

From this perspective, it is no coincidence that the epoch in which human rights have been proclaimed most forcefully is also that in which the wars fought have proved to be the most inhumane. This observation, according to Carl Schmitt, is not at all paradoxical since it is when fighting in the name of humanity that one is justified in considering one's enemies as inhuman. Proclaimed humanism ends in actual dehumanisation. The Kosovo War, conducted in the name of 'human rights,' resulted in a systematic violation of the rights of the Serbs, as well as a considerable amount of 'collateral damage.' The war conducted against Iraq in the name of 'freedom' ended in what General Tommy Franks characterised as a 'catastrophic success.' Another reason is that there cannot be timeless fundamental rights, for what is fundamental is always determined by a specific epoch or culture.[63]

---

61 *Democracy and Leadership* (Indianapolis: Liberty Fund, 1979), p. 337. Originally published in 1924.

62 *Public Papers of the Presidents of the United States, George W. Bush: 2002* (Washington, DC: Office of the Federal Register, National Archives and Records Service, 2004), Book Two, p. 1572.

63 Cf., on this point, Norberto Bobbio, *Il problema della guerra e le vie della pace* (Bologna: Il Mulino, 1970), pp. 119-157. On the political use of the rhetoric of human rights in relation to the thought of Carl Schmitt, cf. also William Rasch, 'Human Rights as Geopolitics: Carl Schmitt and the Legal Form of American Supremacy,' in *Cultural Critique* 54, Spring 2003, pp. 120-147.

Total war marks not only the return to the 'state of nature' as Hobbes imagined it. The wars where the enemy is considered as a criminal or an outlaw thereby betray their theological or religious character. Like the crusades, the wars of religion or wars conducted against the heretics or pagans, these are wars without limits, wars taken to extremes, because they come under moral categories between which there can be no reconciliation. 'It goes without saying,' notes Norbert Campagna, 'that evil cannot enjoy "equality under the law" with the good side: the forces that fight for "the good" lay claim to all of the rights, while the forces that are ranged on the side of "evil" find themselves, for their part, deprived of all rights, for it is inconceivable to let the forces of evil enjoy any rights whatsoever. [...] The "good" can drop bombs on civilian populations; the "bad" have no right to do so. [...] If the cause for which one fights a war is just [then] all hostile acts one commits in it are intrinsically just, however little care one takes to wage it according to the rulebook.'[64] The fight in the name of good authorises not only the interference in the internal affairs of sovereign states (in the name of humanitarianism, freedom, democracy or human rights) but also the restriction of freedoms, the opening of camps that permit the internment of prisoners without any legal status, the bombing of civilian populations, the destruction of industrial infrastructure, the recourse to torture, the use of napalm or white phosphorus, depleted uranium projectiles, cluster bombs, anti-personnel mines, and so on. In a public debate on CBS in 1996, the former Secretary of State, Madeleine Albright, was questioned by Leslie Stahl on the necessity of establishing a blockade against Iraq, thereby bringing about the deaths of 500,000 Iraqi children ('We have heard that a half-million children have died [in Iraq]. I mean, that's more children than died in Hiroshima. Is the price worth it?'). Albright's reply was unequivocal: 'I think this is a very hard choice, but we think the price is worth it.'[65]

The consequences of equating the enemy with a criminal who should be punished, are therefore considerable. 'That ends,' writes Jean François Kervégan, 'in the transformation of international law into an annex of the penal code, and war into a police action aimed at repressing the guilty.'[66] The repression of crimes and offences being

---

64 *Le droit, la politique et la guerre*, pp. 143 and 151.

65 CBS, *60 Minutes*, 12 May 1996.

66 'Carl Schmitt et "l'unité du monde",' p. 11.

traditionally under the jurisdiction of the police, the military gradually assumes the character of a police force. Already in 1904 Theodore
Roosevelt declared that in the future the United States could indeed
find itself forced to 'exercise [the power] of the international police.'[67]
In the period between the wars, at the time of the Kellogg-Briand Pact
(1928), the 'prohibition of war' would lead belligerents to redefine
their interventions as so many international police actions in order
to avoid the criminalisation of their enterprises. Today, notably in the
context of the war on terror, we are witnessing a revealing blurring of
the distinction between police and army: while the police are increasingly made to uphold internal order by military means, the army
undertakes wars which are regularly presented as international police
actions.

In much the same way, the boundary between domestic and foreign politics, that is, between international conflicts and civil wars, is
breaking down. As Claude Polin observes, 'The new wars are and can
only be universal (world wars), merciless (without quarter), unlimited
(total) and without rules (these are international civil wars).'[68] Carl
Schmitt emphasises on many occasions that the just war inevitably
leads to civil war by virtue of the fact that it can be conducted without consideration of the rules of the *jus in bello*. One of the essential
rules of the 'war in due form' is the distinction between combatants
and non-combatants, between soldiers and civilians. This distinction is automatically effaced in the just wars of modern times, where
one tends to consider that the entire enemy population is guilty. The
recourse to indiscriminate aerial bombardment, with its destructive
power and at the same time anonymous and 'cold-blooded' character,
is one of the logical consequences of this development.

Today, we also see the proliferation of non-state actors (non-govern-
mental organisations, private and multinational foundations, financial interests, lobbyists, etc.) in all the domains of international life.
This development has redefined the relationships between the public
and the private spheres, and between the civilian and military sectors.
Whereas soldiers become more and more 'technicians' or 'civilians
in uniform,' we simultaneously see an accelerated privatisation of all

---

67 State of the Union address, 6 December 1904.

68 'La guerre et ses causes: Essai sur l'histoire des formes de la guerre en Occident,' in
    La guerre: Actes du colloque universitaire du 17 mai 2003 (Paris: Association des
    Amis de Guy Augé, 2004), p. 94.

that relates to security (or to preventing insecurity). The privatisation of war does not result merely from the fact that, in many theatres of operation, the belligerents are civilians who have taken up arms, or from the fact that certain criminal organisations now have recourse to veritable private armies, as is the case with certain drug cartels. Another notable fact is the reappearance of private mercenary armies, notably in the United States, where in the absence of conscription, enrolment in the regular army is relatively small in relation to the total population.

The private military companies, or PMCs, independent or not of the military-industrial complex, today occupy a rising position in the architecture of the American military and national security (especially since their use compensates for the reluctance of Congress to put in regular troops on the ground). The turnover of such companies, in some cases listed on the stock market, is constantly growing. The best known are DynCorp Inc., Military Professional Resources Inc. (MPRI), Kellogg Brown & Rott (KBR), Blackwater Security Consulting, Erinys, Sandline, Titan and Caci International. KBR, which belongs to the Halliburton multinational, where several members of the Bush government hold personal interests, signed a 200 million dollar contract with the Pentagon on 13 June 2003. The security company Blackwater has itself deployed almost 50,000 mercenaries around the world. These private companies, which are always looking for new markets related to defence and security, have been pivotal in the redeployment of American power in the Persian Gulf. Today, they are especially active in Iraq, where nearly 20,000 mercenaries provide logistical support for the regular forces, without any excessive care of the choice of means (and without their deaths being counted among the losses suffered by the American military). These auxiliary combatants, who are sometimes paid as much as 1,000 dollars per day, are not subject to any rules, conventions or regulations. Their status is eminently paradoxical for, although legally employed by the United States, under international law they are considered illegal combatants.[69] 'The private military companies employed by the Pentagon (sometimes at unreasonably high costs),' writes Sami Makki, 'have become essential

---

69 Let us recall that the Geneva Convention, which was ratified by the United States, prohibits the employment of mercenaries, who cannot therefore benefit from the protection accorded to regular combatants by the Hague conventions of 1899 and 1907.

for a new interventionist strategy based on the capacity to rapidly deploy forces anywhere in the world.'[70] The mercenary 'market' is today estimated at 100 billion dollars a year.[71] Concomitantly, but in an opposite direction, we see a militarisation of humanitarianism, due to development and humanitarian aid themselves becoming auxiliary instruments in the fight against asymmetric threats, as well as in the expansion of influence on the international scene.

The effacement of boundaries between the classical categories of aggression culminates in the confusion of the notions of war and peace themselves. When the enemy is set up as a figure of evil, it is no longer possible to make peace with him, for to make peace would be to compromise with evil. In the old law of nations (*jus gentium*), defeat was considered sufficient 'punishment.' Now, one has to impeach before tribunals those whom one stigmatises as 'responsible' for the war. The indefinite pursuit of war, even in times of peace, then becomes a moral imperative. Carl Schmitt saw that the Treaty of Versailles and the Kellogg-Briand Pact created an intermediate state between war and peace in which peace became a sort of pursuit of war by other means.[72] This situation has not ceased to evolve ever since, ending

---

70 *Militarisation de l'humanitaire, privatisation du militaire, et stratégie globale des Etats-Unis* (Paris: Centre interdisciplinaire de recherches sur la paix et d'études stratégiques [CIRPES], 2004), p. 13. According to the bulletin *Foreign Report*, published by the Jane's Information Group, out of an initial budget of 85 billion dollars released by the American administration for the military operations in the Near East, $28 billion have been spent on mercenaries or individuals serving in paramilitary forces.

71 Cf. Peter Singer, *Corporate Warriors: The Rise of the Privatized Military Industry* (Ithaca: Cornell University Press, 2003); Philippe Chapleau, *Sociétés militaires privées: Enquête sur les soldats sans armées* (Paris: Rocher, 2005); Jean-Jacques Roche (ed.), *Insécurités publiques, sécurité privée? Essais sur les nouveaux mercenaires* (Paris: Economica, 2005); Olivier Hubac (ed.), *Mercenaires et polices privées: La privatisation de la violence armée* (Paris: Universalis, 2006); Xavier Renou, *La privatisation de la violence: Mercenaires et sociétés privées au service du marché* (Marseilles: Agone, 2006). On the privatisation of espionage, cf. Jean-Jacques Cécile, *Espionnage business: Guerre économique et renseignement* (Paris: Ellipses, 2005).

72 'Where it is no longer possible,' writes Carl Schmitt, 'to discern what is war and what is peace, it becomes even more difficult to say what neutrality is' (*La notion de politique*, p. 172). Cf., on this subject, Aurélie de Andrade, 'La distinction temps de paix/temps de guerre en droit pénal militaire: quelques éléments de compréhension,' in *Les Champs de Mars*, Second quarter 2001, pp. 155-169, who emphasises the way in which the emergence and the development of an international criminal code have accentuated this tendency further. 'We are forced to note,' she writes, 'the absence of the distinction between wartime and peacetime in the international criminal code. Whether it be in the statutes and regulations of the two international

up as near-indistinguishability. The 'just war' of modern times no longer ends in a peace treaty in good and due form, but is pursued *in peace* under other forms. Once the guns have fallen silent, the guilty should still be punished, while the enemy population should possibly be 'reeducated.' The wars no longer end: they become interminable, for it becomes much more difficult to put an end to them when they are pursued also in peace. 'Cold war' or 'hot war': aggression becomes, under different forms, a permanent condition. It is at the same time an eradication of the border between the exception (which is war) and the norm (which is peace). Finally, given that according to Carl Schmitt, politics implies the recognition of the enemy, Clausewitz's classic formula that war is the continuation of politics by other means is reversed: war becomes instead 'the destruction of politics by every means.'[73]

This erosion of the border between war and peace is much more damaging to the concept of peace than the concept of war. There are two reasons for this. First, because the concept of peace cannot be interpreted in as many ways as the concept of war (there is at most only one form of peace while there are numerous forms of war). And second, one wages war to obtain peace and not peace to obtain war, and the end should always be more clearly defined than the means of arriving at it.

There is no doubt that Carl Schmitt's critique of the 'just war' of modern times concerns primarily the United States of America, for the vast majority of wars conducted by this country have not been regulated wars, 'duel wars,' but wars conducted against enemies treated as criminals and pursued until their total capitulation. For

---

penal tribunals of the Hague and Arusha or in that of the International Criminal Court, there is no trace of this distinction' (p.189). The adaptation of the French penal code and military law to the statute of these new judiciary authorities can consequently only 'bring about, if not the disappearance, at least an attenuation of the distinction between peacetime and wartime' (ibid.) This tendency had been remarked already in the 1960s by Jules Monnerot: 'The end of the battle, end in the double sense of the word, being able to be only victory, the official distinction between war and peace, with its train of conventions [...], if not abolished, at least does not have the deep adherence of the new converts, who admit it only on the tactical level because they cannot do otherwise, and do not morally disarm in the time-intervals separating two "limited wars": politics is the "continuation of war by other means", we shall say, inverting Clausewitz' (*Inquisitions*, [Paris: José Corti, 1974], pp. 95-96).

73 *De defensa*, 25 October 2004, p. 19.

Carl Schmitt, 'All significant concepts of the modern theory of the state are secularized theological concepts.'[74] ('*Alle prägnanten Begriffe der modernen Staatslehre sind säkularisierte theologische Begriffe.*') In certain respects, 'political theology' is more prevalent in the United States inasmuch as the privileged position that an omnipresent civil religion occupies there explains to a large extent the messianic nature of American foreign policy, a character that transcends the divide between Republicans and Democrats (and even between interventionists and isolationists).

Herman Melville, in the nineteenth century, declared in his novel *White Jacket*: '[W]e Americans are the peculiar, chosen people — the Israel of our time; we bear the ark of the liberties of the world. [...] God has given to us, for a future inheritance, the broad domains of the political pagans [...] we are the pioneers of the world.'[75] Invoked in the United States during the entire second half of that century, the doctrine of a 'manifest destiny' enunciated in 1845 by Sean O'Sullivan, realises the fusion of imperialism and divine election, giving at one stroke a religious and moral legitimacy to political, cultural and commercial conquest.[76] Senator Albert J. Beveridge would later say: 'God has not been preparing the English-speaking and Teutonic peoples for a thousand years for nothing but vain and idle self-contemplation and self-admiration. No! He has made us the master organizers of the world to establish system where chaos reigns.'[77] This viewpoint, which goes back to the Pilgrim Fathers and the myth of the 'city on a hill,' has never died out. One could cite innumerable examples of it. The promised New World, the United States, believes in its universal values and, considering itself to be invested with a divine mission, seeks in good conscience to impose them on the rest of the world.[78] Did Ronald Reagan not declare already in 1980, 'Can we doubt that only a

---

74   Carl Schmitt, *Political Theology*, p. 36.

75   *White Jacket; or, the World in a Man-of-War* (London: Richard Bentley, 1850), vol. 1, pp. 238-239.

76   Cf. Anders Stephenson, *Manifest Destiny, America Expansion and the Empire of Right* (New York: Hill & Wang, 1995).

77   Cited by Claude G. Bowers, *Beveridge and the Progressive Era* (New York: Houghton Mifflin, 1932), p. 121.

78   Cf. Clifford Longley, *Chosen People: The Big Idea that Shapes England and America* (London: Hodder & Stoughton, 2002); Stephen H. Webb, *American Providence: A Nation with a Mission* (New York: Continuum, 2004): and Fuad Sha'ban, *For Zion's Sake: The Judeo-Christian Tradition in American Culture* (London: Pluto Press, 2005).

Divine Providence placed this land, this island of freedom, here as a refuge for all those people in the world who yearn to breathe freely?'[79] Bill Clinton too declared during the inaugural speech of his second term, that 'America stands alone as the world's indispensable nation.'

Thanks to the events of 11 September 2001, the collusion between the neoconservatives and the Protestant churches of evangelical affiliation has been accentuated in a revealing manner. The messianic vision inherited from Puritanism and the Calvinist doctrine of pre-destination, which cemented the consensus of the American society for a long time, has undergone a flowering. The myth of America as the 'chosen nation,' charged with imposing Good all over the world and against which the forces of Evil shall not prevail, since Providence presided at its birth, has again come to the fore, as in the epoch of the Great Awakening between 1730 and 1750, with unusual force not only in the political and diplomatic domains, but also in the geopo-litical. 'Our nationalism,' writes William Kristol and David Brooks, 'is that of an exceptional nation founded on a universal principle, on what Lincoln called "an abstract truth, applicable to all men and all times."'[80] This vision is consolidated by the certitude of being a bearer of what is best in political and social matters: 'Americans should not deny the fact that of all the nations in the history of the world, theirs is the most just [...] and the best model for the future.'[81] 'If the United States represents a people chosen by God,' observes Kenneth M. Coleman, 'then it is almost impossible to conceive a situation in which the interests of humanity are not eminently similar to those of the United States.'[82] 'There is a value system that cannot be compromised, and that is the values we praise. And if the values are good enough for our people, they ought to be good enough for others,' one could recently read in *The Washington Post*.[83] Many more similar state-ments could be cited. Such an atmosphere tends to end in a fusion of

---

79 From Reagan's acceptance speech for the presidential nomination at the Republican National Convention, 17 July 1980.

80 *The Wall Street Journal*, 15 September 1997.

81 David Rothkopf, 'In Praise of Cultural Imperialism?,' in *Foreign Policy*, Summer 1997.

82 *The Political Mythology of the Monroe Doctrine: Reflection on the Social Psychology of Domination*, n.d., p. 105.

83 *Washington Post*, 19 November 2002. (It should be noted that this was said by President George W. Bush.-Ed.)

nationalism and messianism: 'From the armed hand of the Christian Messiah, Uncle Sam is becoming the Messiah himself.'[84]

This messianic certitude of incarnating the good, this tendency to posit the American principles as universal, makes of America a 'virtuous empire,' where Claes G. Ryn has, paradoxically, been able to discern the mark of a 'new Jacobinism.'[85] This 'Jacobinism' consists in wishing to bring all societies into alignment with the American model, in causing all different political cultures to disappear in favour of a global 'market democracy.' John Gray takes the view that American foreign policy is based on the ideological conviction that 'the market state' is the only legitimate mode of government, even though it is a specifically American construct.[86] In fact, it has often been emphasised how many Americans have a tendency to confuse the United States with the world—a world considered understandable only after it has been Americanised. Historically, universalism has always favoured expansionism and colonialism. The colonial conquests were officially motivated by the desire to spread the principles of 'civilisation' and 'progress' to the world, both principles being identified with a particular culture professing to be 'universal.' The values or aspirations proper for one particular nation thus became identified with moral laws supposed to govern the universe: a particular national interest became universalised to the point of becoming, theoretically, the interest of all humanity. From this way of looking at things it follows that the colonised are colonised for their own good, and that it is in the interest of the dominated to be dominated. In such a perspective every refusal to adopt the model posited as the best is quite naturally interpreted as a manifestation of foolishness or perverse hostility. This is an intrinsically war-engendering interpretation: 'Because the ideology of virtuous empire envisions not only American world dominance but the remaking of the world in its image,' writes Ryn, 'it is a recipe for conflict and perpetual war.'[87]

Feeling threatened by everything that is different from itself, the United States basically strives for a world without enemies and

---

84 *Dieu bénisse l'Amérique: La religion de la Maison-Blanche,* p. 248. Cf. also Tarek Mitri, *Au nom de la Bible, au nom de l'Amérique* (Geneva: Labor et Fides, 2004).

85 *America the Virtuous: The Crisis of Democracy and the Quest for Empire* (New Brunswick: Transaction, 2003).

86 *Al Qaeda and What it Means to be Modern* (London: Faber, 2003), p. 95.

87 'History and the Moral Order,' p. 22.

threats, which must inevitably be the equivalent to a homogeneous world. They think that they will not be truly safe until everything that is fundamentally different has been eliminated, that is, when the entire world has been Americanised. Their unilateralism, even more than their isolationism, cannot be otherwise explained.

Already during the signing of the Kellogg-Briand Pact, the United States (which had refused to join the League of Nations), had explained that it reserved the right to be the sole judge of what constituted a war of aggression and of what justified the recognition or non-recognition of a state. Much more recently, in April 2001, it withdrew from the United Nations Commission on Human Rights. In November 2001, it confirmed its refusal to ratify the international convention, already signed and ratified by 144 countries, which prohibits the manufacture, acquisition and stocking of biological arms, for the sole reason that it does not accept the inspection or checking of its laboratories and its arsenals. Some days later, it unilaterally revoked the Anti-Ballistic Missile Treaty of 1972, which limits the deployment of anti-missile defences. It also refused to sign the treaty prohibiting anti-person-nel mines, signed in February 2001 by 123 countries, as well as the Kyoto treaty on the protection of the environment and global warm-ing. In May 2001, it refused all discussion with its European partners concerning the spying and eavesdropping network 'Echelon.' It still opposes the whole world on the production of genetically modified organisms (GMOs) and hormone-enriched meat. It is also the only Western country which has never ratified the convention on the elim-ination of all forms of discrimination against women adopted in 1979 by the United Nations, nor the convention of 1989 on the rights of children. It has made known that it does not recognise, in respect of its citizens, the authority of the International Court of Justice of the Hague, whose creation it financed. Finally, it was without the endorse-ment of the United Nations, and in opposition to the vast majority of the countries of the international community, that it decided to attack, invade and occupy Iraq.

On all these issues, particularly since George W. Bush became president, the United States thus appears determined to evade inter-national norms and exempt itself from rules it intends to apply or have applied to others. It thus posits itself as an *exceptional country* — as a country which, by its very nature, should enjoy freedom not to observe any of the laws which it wishes others to observe. In such a perspective it can only reject as restrictive, obsolete, or irrelevant the rules which, in the best of cases, it admits only insofar as they are not applied to itself. That is why it ever more frequently adopts a strictly unilateral attitude. There is no doubt that in its eyes it is the rest of the world that must adapt.

Even when, as we have just seen, it considers that its nationals cannot be subjected to international criminal proceedings, the United States at the same time contends that citizens of other countries are subject to its laws.[88] In this way it transforms criminal law into a means of affirming its sovereignty. 'Like every nation-state,' Jean-Claude Paye writes, 'the United States establishes a double juridical system, a state of law for the nationals and a state devoid of law for foreigners. Classically, for the other nations, the distinction between the two juridical orders is articulated at the border. However, for the American state, the border is not a geographical fact. The primacy of American nationality and the organisation of the two juridical orders do not operate on a determined territory, but in the whole world. It is a question not only of permitting American citizens to escape from international tribunals, that is to say, from common jurisdictions, but also to make the other states recognise the right of the American authorities to judge the nationals of these countries by exceptional jurisdiction, specially created for this purpose.'[89]

As we have seen, the United States does not hesitate to designate the enemy, which unquestionably seems very Schmittian. It does this with a determination and an energy which contrasts with the softness and indecision that the European countries often evince. But this designation of the enemy does not at all correspond to the criteria enunciated by Carl Schmitt. Not only does it not represent for the US the political gesture par excellence—which, as such, could only be evaluated by political criteria—but it assumes an immediately Manichaean and moral dimension. The enemy of America is not someone whom circumstances has made into an adversary, and who under other circumstances could be transformed into an ally. He is identified with Evil.

---

88 The extradition treaties signed on 25 June 2003 between the European Union and the United States sanction the material integration of the European judiciary apparatuses into the American system of war against terrorism.

89 'Le droit pénal comme un acte constituent: Une mutation du droit pénal,' p. 286.

In his speech of 3 August 1983, Ronald Reagan had already designated the USSR and the countries of the Eastern bloc as 'the evil empire.' Since then, the Soviet system has been replaced by other enemies; 'international terrorism' and 'rogue states,' according to the expression coined in 1994 by Madeleine Albright, but the enemy continues to be denounced in the same terms. After the attacks of 11 September, George W. Bush immediately chose to present the war against terrorism as a 'battle of good and evil' ('Good and evil rarely manifest themselves as clearly').[90] He asked the rest of the world to stand by him in his 'crusade' ('Join us in our crusade or face the certain prospect of death and destruction'). Evoking the attacks on New York and Washington, he declared: 'Today, our nation saw evil.'[91] On 29 January 2002, the American president also used David Frum's expression the 'axis of evil' that would subsequently be repeated several times. According to this point of view, the world is divided into those who fight for good and those who oppose it or who are accomplices of evil. There is no third position, no possibility of remaining neutral. 'Either you are with us, or you are with the terrorists,' George W. Bush declared before Congress on 20 September 2002.[92]

What is very remarkable is that this Manichaean system, which conceives of the world as a battlefield that is irremediably divided into two camps, that of Good and that of Evil, is today found both in the speeches of Osama bin Laden and in those of Bush — and doubtlessly made in good faith in both cases. The principal terrorist, bin Laden, calls for 'jihad' against the 'great Satan,' George W. Bush for a 'crusade' against the 'axis of evil.' The parallels are striking. At first glance, both the American president and bin Laden adhere to the idea that the world and politics can be understood only in terms of friends and enemies.[93] But there too, one would be wrong to infer any sort of

---

90   It should be noted that this quote has been attributed to an unspecified 'American newscaster,' and was never said by President Bush.-Ed.

91   Said in his address on the evening of 11 September 2001.

92   Cf. Andrew Norris, '"Us" and "Them",' in *Metaphilosophy* XXXV, 3, April 2004, pp. 249-272, which examines the reaction of the Bush administration to the attacks of 11 September and its way of diabolising the enemy in the light of works published by Schmitt in the twenties.

93   On this subject, cf. Darius Rejali, 'Friend and Enemy, East or West: Political Realism in the Work of Usama bin Ladin, Carl Schmitt, Niccolo Machiavelli and Kai-ka'us ibn Iskandar,' in *Historical Reflections* 3, 2004, pp. 425-443. Cf. also for what concerns Iran, William O. Beeman, *The 'Great Satan' vs. the 'Mad Mullahs': How the United States and Iran Demonize Each Other* (Greenwood: Praeger, 2005).

influence of the thought of Carl Schmitt. For the way in which the two of them pose the question of enmity is in no way Schmittian, since they pose it in absolute terms and eliminate from it the possibility of third parties which could remain neutral. In other words, they believe not only in the inevitability of a conflictual dimension in political life, they believe that this conflictuality opposes only two camps against each other and that it should be immediately carried to extremes. The characteristic element is the religious aspect, which is found in both speeches (each of the two protagonists of course refusing to recognise this aspect in his adversary, as for Bush, bin Laden is merely a criminal while, for bin Laden, Bush is merely the representative of a decadent materialistic world, even if he is also a 'crusader'). Jacques Derrida has correctly observed that the Bush-bin Laden confrontation funda-mentally brings into play 'two political theologies.'[94] Bruno Etienne, a specialist on Islam, has made the same observation: 'The jihad is opposed to the crusade, Good to Evil, Allah to the Great Satan, the Afghan *fatwa* to the "Texan *fatwa*"; in short, we are confronted with a fratricidal war opposing God to God.'[95] Carlo Galli, an excellent expert on Carl Schmitt, speaks similarly of 'apocalyptic theology.'[96] Islamic fundamentalism on one side, neoconservative fundamental-ism on the other.

With the attacks of September 11, the United States in any case realised that it is was henceforth vulnerable on its own soil. The recog-nition of this vulnerability, contrasting with its (justified) conviction of possessing 'a position of unparalleled military strength and great economic and political influence,'[97] has brought about a redefinition of its strategic objectives and of its modes of operation.

The new American strategy was officially stated in a public report issued in September 2002. There it is made clear already in the first

---

94 'Autoimmunità, suicidi reali e simbolici,' interview of October 2001 published in Giovanna Borradori, *Filosofia del terrore: Dialoghi con Jürgen Habermas e Jacques Derrida* (Rome: Laterza, 2003), p. 126 (English: 'Autoimmunity: Real and Symbolic Suicides: A Dialogue with Jacques Derrida,' in *Philosophy in a Time of Terror: Dialogues with Jürgen Habermas and Jacques Derrida* [Chicago: University of Chicago Press, 2003], p. 117); French: *Le 'concept' du 11 septembre: Dialogues à New York, octobre-décembre 2001* [Paris: Galilée, 2004]).

95 Cited by François Heisbourg, *Iperterrorismo: La nuova guerra*, 2002, p. 53.

96 *La guerra globale* (Rome: Laterza, 2002), p. 27.

97 *The National Security Strategy of the United States of America* (Washington, DC: White House, 2002), p. iv.

pages that the United States will no longer accept that its enemies may attack first: 'As a matter of common sense and self-defense, America will act against such emerging threats before they are fully formed.'[98] 'We must adapt the concept of imminent threat to the capabilities and objectives of today's adversaries,' the report also states.[99] Contrary to strategies based on retaliation or defence, the precautionary attack thus becomes the rule. It is no longer a question of waiting for the threat to materialise; it should be prevented or anticipated by attacking first. George W. Bush indicated as much already in a speech made in June 2002 before the Military Academy at West Point.

These orientations have been confirmed by the report entitled *The National Defense Strategy of the United States of America*, published by the Department of Defense in March 2005, where one may read: '[W]e will defeat adversaries at the time, place, and in the manner of our choosing — setting the conditions for future security.'[100] The text underlines that 'America is a nation at war' and that '[t]he attacks of 9/11 gave us greater clarity on the challenges that confront us.'[101]It is made clear that the sovereignty of countries that represent a 'threat' will not be respected.[102] The 'problem states' are defined as those that are 'hostile to U.S. principles.' The document reaffirms the principle of preventive war against the 'entities [who] are hostile to freedom, democracy, and other U.S. interests':[103] 'Allowing opponents to strike first [...] is unacceptable. Therefore, the United States must defeat the most dangerous challenges early and at a safe distance, before they are allowed to mature.'[104] Cyberspace, finally, is defined as a 'new theater of operations.'[105]

The problem is that this doctrine of 'legitimate preventive defence' contradicts Article 51 of the Charter of the United Nations, under which defensive wars are only legitimate in response to an attack by another state, thus totally excluding the 'pre-emptive' attack, even

---

98   The *National Security Strategy of the United States of America*, p. v.

99   The *National Security Strategy of the United States of America*, p. 15.

100 The *National Defense Strategy of the United States of America* (U.S. Dept. of Defense, 2005), p. iv.

101 The *National Defense Strategy of the United States of America*, p. 1.

102 The *National Defense Strategy of the United States of America*, p. 1.

103 The *National Defense Strategy of the United States of America*, p. 8.

104 The *National Defense Strategy of the United States of America*, p. 9.

105 The *National Defense Strategy of the United States of America*, p. 13.

when based on the supposed existence of an 'imminent threat.' The prohibition of the use of force except in cases of legitimate defence and in respect of actions carried out at the behest, and under the auspices, of the Security Council, figures equally in Article 2 of the Charter of the United Nations. The reason for this prohibition is that preventive wars have always been considered wars of aggression under modern international law.

In the domain of international affairs, the application of this doctrine has been translated into the war in Afghanistan, followed by the second Iraq War, undertaken in a 'preventive' way, in violation of all the rules of international law and without the support of the United Nations. At the same time, the United States has also put its allies under strong pressure in order to make them, too, disregard principles of international law, and even their own constitutions — albeit most of them refused — in accordance with the principle 'who is not with us is against us.'

For the Bush administration, military power appears to be more important than politics, diplomacy and even economics as a means of exercising influence and imposing hegemony. Becoming increasingly a permanent means, war tends to become an end in itself, making the sociopolitical necessity of a peace treaty superfluous. At the same time, the American military power becomes ubiquitous, that is to say, capable of intervening everywhere and at any time due to the global range attained by intercontinental ballistic missiles, which allows the projection of power to any point on the globe thanks to a sophisticated logistics of expeditionary capacities (networks of aerial and naval bases, the militarisation of space, precision targeting, prepositioned modular stocks, systematic recourse to information technology, etc.). The doctrine of preventive war, finally, reveals the sovereign. To express it in Schmittian terms: to speak of a 'rogue state' comes down to saying that the one who decides unilaterally who is a 'rogue' is the sovereign.

In America, preventive war has often been presented either as a sort of legitimate defence by anticipation, or as a military form of the 'precautionary principle.' It comes down to punishing a virtual or supposed 'crime' even before it has been committed, which opens the door to all sorts of speculations concerning the intention of committing it attributed to the 'threatening' nations. One of the science-fiction novels of Philip K. Dick entitled *Minority Report* (from which a successful film was derived) imagines a future society in which murderers can be arrested and placed in detention even before committing their crimes. The preventive 'strategy' of the United States is a sort of extension of this principle, and runs up against the same problems that a would-be murderer or terrorist whom one arrests before he has committed the act, is strictly speaking, if not 'innocent,' at least someone who has not yet done anything at the moment when he is deprived of his freedom. This strategy thus comes down to rendering people who have not broken the law harmless on the grounds that one is convinced that they had the intention of breaking it. From that point arises the problem of evaluation and of proof: how does one demonstrate an intention? And how does one reply to those who contest this evaluation? As Francesco Ragazzi writes, 'the only possible justification of intervention would be the infallible character of prediction.'[106] But how could it be infallible? To justify the war against Iraq it was alleged that the regime of Saddam Hussein possessed 'weapons of mass destruction' and had the intention of using them. We know today that this was only an official lie.[107]

The adoption of a doctrine of preventive war by the United States and of the right to attack first marks a manifest rupture with the rules of modern international law, and seems in fact to attest to a will to return to the model of the medieval 'just war.'[108] 'The aim of the argu-

---

106 '"The National Security Strategy of the USA" ou la rencontre improbable de Grotius, Carl Schmitt et Philip K. Dick,' in *Cultures et conflits*, 18 May 2005. Cf. also Betty Glad and Chris J. Dolan (eds.), *Striking First: The Pre-Emption and Preventive War Doctrines and the Reshaping of U.S. Foreign Policy* (Basingstoke: Palgrave, 2005).

107 Donald Rumsfeld also eventually recognised that there was no evidence proving the alleged links between Al Qaeda and Saddam Hussein's Iraq (*The Guardian*, 6 October 2004).

108 The concept of 'just war' has been the object of a redefinition and a positive reevaluation on the part of Michael Walzer (*Just and Unjust Wars: A Moral Argument with Historical Illustrations* [New York: Basic Books, 1977], French translation: *Guerres justes et injustes: Argumentation morale avec exemples historiques* (Paris: Belin, 1999); *Arguing about War* (New Haven: Yale University Press, 2003), French translation: *De la guerre et du terrorisme* (Paris: Bayard, 2004). This redefinition is quite close to that proposed by Monique Canto-Sperber in *Le Bien, la guerre et la terreur. Pour une morale internationale* (Paris: Plon, 2005), who strains to make a distinction between 'just war' and 'moral war.' The manifesto of the American intellectuals (Samuel Huntington, Francis Fukuyama, Michael Walzer, etc.) favourable to the war in Iraq published on 1 October 2002 by The Institute for American Values ('What We're Fighting For') itself places the war against terrorism within the framework of the just war, but without ever considering the limits placed on its operations or the balance to be established between military repression and military means. On this subject, cf. also William Rasch, 'A Just War? Or Just a War? Schmitt, Habermas, and the Cosmopolitan Orthodoxy,' in Andreas Kalyvas and Jan

ments of the White House,' writes Francesco Ragazzi, 'is indeed to pass off an act recognised from the beginning as illegal for something that would be one of the characteristics of the "just war."'[109] That is, however, impossible, for the classical definition of the 'just war,' in Grotius for example, formally excludes the first attack and preventive wars prompted by fear of a supposed attack.[110] For the old theoreticians of the just war, war is, at the same time, always an (inevitable) evil, in certain circumstances a (possible) lesser evil and a (legitimate) remedy against evil. In spite of its 'moral' background, the just war, as we have seen above, continues to obey certain principles and observe certain conditions. Everything is therefore not permitted in it: the existence itself of the *jus in bello* contradicts the adage *inter arma silent leges* ('in times of war, the law falls silent'), legitimate defence being itself defined in very strict terms.

Müller (eds.), *Carl Schmitt: Legacy and Prospects, An International Conference in New York City*, special issue of the *Cardozo Law Review* XXI, 5/6, May 2000, pp. 1665-1684; Slavoj Žižek, 'Are We in a War? Do We Have an Enemy?,' in *The London Review of Books* XXIV, 10, May 2002; Fabio Vander, *Kant, Schmitt e la guerre preventive: Diritto e politica nell'epoca del conflitto globale* (Rome: Manifesto libri, 2004); Chris Brown, 'From Humanised War to Humanitarian Intervention: Carl Schmitt's Critique of the Just War Tradition,' paper at the colloquium *The International Thought of Carl Schmitt*, The Hague, 9-11 September 2004; Mark Evans (ed.), *Just War Theory: A Reappraisal* (New York: Palgrave Macmillan, 2005); S. C. Roach, 'Decisionism and Humanitarian Intervention: Reinterpreting Carl Schmitt and the Global Political Order,' in *Alternatives* XXX, 2005, 4, pp. 443-460; and Sigrid Weigel, 'The Critique of Violence or, The Challenge to Political Theology of Just Wars and Terrorism with a Religious Face,' in *Telos* 135, Summer 2006, pp. 61-76.

109 '"The National Security Strategy of the USA" ou la rencontre improbable de Grotius, Carl Schmitt et Philip K. Dick.'

110 'Quite untenable is the position, which has been maintained by some,' writes Grotius, 'that according to the law of nations it is right to take up arms in order to weaken a growing power which, if it becomes too great, may be a source of danger' (Stephen C. Neff [ed.], *Hugo Grotius on the Law of War and Peace* [Cambridge: Cambridge University Press, 2012], p. 90). This is the reason why Yaron Brook and Alex Epstein ('"Just War Theory" vs. American Self-Defense,' in *The Objective Standard* I, 1, Spring 2006) criticise the concept of 'just war': in their eyes it is too restrictive! Citing as examples to be imitated the terror bombardments of Germany during the Second World War and the massacre of the civilian populations of Georgia by the Union General William T. Sherman in 1864, Brook and Epstein reject the very concept of 'proportionality' between attack and defence and go so far as to accuse the Bush administration of 'defeatism' for not having engaged straightaway in a total war against militant Islam. 'In Afghanistan and in Iraq,' they write, 'we have seen the consequences of the non-adoption of a Sherman-like policy.' The two authors, who qualify the use of torture in this context as 'morally obligatory,' profess the philosophy of 'rational egoism' enunciated by Ayn Rand.

The concept of just war also leads to the question of who is author-ised to determine whether a war is just or not. Who decides on the conformity to 'justice' in such a circumstance? In the Middle Ages, such decisions were generally referred to a third party deemed to be impartial. But George W. Bush rejects forthwith the idea of such a third party (which could be the United Nations), just as he rejects the idea of neutrality. As long as the task of characterising a war is not referred to a third party, only the dominant power is capable of validating the idea that a military enterprise is justified or not, in which case the 'just war' is nothing more than the war waged by the strongest.

If the doctrine of the just war is making a comeback today, based on the ideology of human rights, that is, on the modern version of subjec-tive natural law, it is in a 'wild' manner, without taking into account the principles used in the Middle Ages to determine if a war was 'just' or 'unjust.' From now on it suffices for a war to be declared just (by those who conduct it), that it be conducted in the name of the grand principles of freedom, humanity or democracy, even if these princi-ples themselves are constantly flouted in the course of the hostilities. The other conditions are lost sight of. More than in the medieval wars, this type of war, of a strongly ideological and moral character, rather reminds us of the wars of extermination that are narrated in the Bible. The rhetoric of the 'axis of evil' opposed to the forces of good leads us, from this point of view, to the most primitive political theology. As Danilo Zolo writes, 'The new war is "global" in a sense that one can say is *monotheistic* by virtue of the constant references to universal values on the part of the (Western) powers who promote it: war is no longer justified in the name of particular interests or objectives but from a superior and impartial point of view and by invoking values that are supposed to be shared by all of humanity. The Weberian "polythe-ism" of morals and religious beliefs is systematically denied by the theoreticians of global war. A monotheistic vision of the world — par-ticularly the biblical and ardently Christian one of the present group directing the United States, composed of Methodists, Presbyterians, Episcopalians and Lutherans — is opposed to the pluralism of values and the complexity of the world.'[111]

This procedure permits the United States to posit its sovereignty as inviolable even while considering itself as authorised to intervene as it

---

111 'Una "guerra globale" monoteistica.'

pleases in the rest of the world — and this at the risk of being regarded as the principal factor of the growing brutalisation of international relations. 'The international state of emergency,' writes Francesco Ragazzi, 'would thus be this logic implicit in the American strategy of suspending international norms while making a pretence of carrying out actions which have the force of law [...]. It is a question of submitting other states to a restructured system of international law without submitting to it oneself.'[112] 'It is a question for the United States,' he adds, 'of arrogating to itself the right of suspending the rules of international law to fight against an internal enemy, but internal only in relation to the vague limits drawn by American hegemony, where the entire world becomes the container of what is deemed to be internal.'[113]

The new 'pre-emptive' strategy of the Bush administration is in fact a continuation of neither the old moral Wilsonianism nor of balance-of-power 'realism.' It of course borrows from the first its essentially moral conviction of a 'universal mission' assigned to the chosen nation, from the second the concern for a politics oriented towards the defence of 'the national interest' of the United States, but it constitutes above all a mixed novelty, grounded in unilateralist hegemonism, whose implementation, equivalent to reintroducing the *jus ad omnia*[114] in a selective manner into international politics, entails not the modification but the complete destruction of the written and unwritten rules that constitute international law.[115]

---

112 '"The National Security Strategy of the USA" ou la rencontre improbable de Grotius, Carl Schmitt et Philip K. Dick.'

113 Ibid. Geminello Preterossi, who also speaks of a 'global state of emergency,' considers for his part that the United States tends to establish itself as 'guardians of the world' in the sense in which Schmitt was able to speak of a 'guardian of the constitution' (*L'Occidente contro se stesso*, [Rome: Laterza, 2004], pp. 39-56). Paul Virilio prefers to interpret the recourse to preventive war by reference to the omnipresence of fear in the midst of the postmodern societies. 'The preventive war of George Bush,' he writes, 'is an act of panic by the Pentagon [...]. The preventive war is, in fact, a war lost in advance. To attack preventively proves that one is not sure of oneself. America and its hyperpower are in fact impotent in relation to the novelty of the strategic event. [...] This is a hysterical situation' ('L'état d'urgence permanent,' in *Le Nouvel Observateur*, 26 February 2004, p. 96). (Cf. also Armand Clesse, 'America's Classical Security Dilemma: Search for a New World Order,' in *World Affairs*, April-June 2004, pp. 14-20; and Frederik Rosén, 'Towards a Theory of Institutionalized Judicial Exceptionalism,' in *Journal of Scandinavian Studies in Criminology and Crime Prevention* VI, 2, December 2005, pp. 147-163.)

114 Latin: 'the right to do everything.'

115 Cf. Carlo Galli, *La guerra globale*.

2. FROM PARTISAN TO 'GLOBAL' TERRORIST

At the end of the nineties, Georgy Arbatov, advisor to Gorbachev, declared to the Americans: 'We are going to deal you the most terrible blow: we are going to deprive you of an enemy.' Significant words. The disappearance of the Soviet 'evil empire' risked in fact eliminating the ideological legitimation of the basis for American hegemony over its allies. From then on it was necessary for the Americans to find an alternative enemy, the threat of which — real or supposed, but in any case capable of being exaggerated and exploited — would permit it to continue to impose this hegemony over its partners (more or less transformed into subjects). The United States did that in 2003, two years after the attacks of 11 September by introducing the notion of a global war on terrorism.

This new designation of the enemy explains why numerous authors have undertaken, in the course of these last years, to examine the situation of the present-day world in the light of this or that aspect of the work of Carl Schmitt, in most cases with reference to the military operations conducted by America and the measures taken by Washington to combat Islamism or global terrorism.[116] This is what

---

116 Cf., notably, Thomas Assheuer, 'Geistige Wiederbewaffnung: Nach den Terroranschlägen erlebt der Staatsrechtler Carl Schmitt eine Renaissance,' in *Die Zeit*, 15 November 2001, p. 54; 'Carl Schmitt Revival Designed to Justify Emergency Rule,' in *Executive Intelligence Review* 3, 2001, pp. 69-72; J. Hacke, 'Mit Carl Schmitt in den Krieg — mit Carl Schmitt gegen den Krieg,' in *Ästhetik und Kommunikation* XXXIII, 2002, 118, pp. 29-32; Frederik Stjernfelt, 'Suverænitetens paradokser: Schmitt og terrorisme,' in *Weekendavisen*, 10 May 2002; Nuno Rogeiro, *O inimigo publico: Carl Schmitt, Bin Laden e o terrorismo pós-moderno* (Rio de Janeiro: Gradiva, 2003); Lon Troyer, 'Counterterrorism: Sovereignty, Law, Subjectivity,' in *Critical Asian Studies*, 2003, 2; Ulrich Thiele, 'Der Pate: Carl Schmitt und die Sicherheitsstrategie der USA,' in *Blätter für deutsche und internationale Politik*, August 2004, pp. 992-1000; William Rasch, 'Carl Schmitt and the New World Order,' in *South Atlantic Quarterly* 2, 2004, pp. 177-184; Carsten Bagge Lausten, 'Fjender til døden: en schmittiansk analyse af 11. September og tiden efter,' in *Grus* 71, 2004, pp. 128-146; Peter Stirk, 'Carl Schmitt, the Law of Occupation, and the Iraq War,' in *Constellations* 4, 2004, pp. 527-536 (text reprinted in Peter Stirk, *Carl Schmitt, Crown Jurist of the Third Reich: On Preemptive War, Military*

we ourselves shall do in studying the figure of the 'global' terrorist in comparison with the figure of the partisan, evoked by Carl Schmitt in his famous work *The Theory of the Partisan.*[117]

Occupation, and World Empire [Lewiston: Edwin Mellen Press, 2005], pp. 115-129); Alfred C. Goodson, '"Kosmopiraten," "Kosmopartisanen": Carl Schmitt's Prophetic Partisan,' in *ABLIS Jahrbuch für europäische Prozesse,* vol. 3; *Aufbruch in den rechtsfreien Raum: Normvirulenz als kulturelle Ressource,* 2004, 6 S.; Andreas Behnke, '9/11 und die Grenzen des Politischen,' in *Zeitschrift für internationale Politik* XII, 2005, 1; Francesco Merlo, 'Se questa è una guerra — Sulla "teoria del partigiano" di Carl Schmitt,' in *La Repubblica,* 21 July 2005; and William E. Scheuerman, 'Carl Schmitt and the Road to Abu Ghraib,' in *Constellations* XIII, 1, March 2006, pp. 108-124. William Rasch also strove to translate the theses of Schmitt on conflict in terms borrowed from Luhman and Lyotard ('Conflict as a Vocation: Carl Schmitt and the Possibility of Politics,' in *Theory, Culture and Society,* December 2000, pp. 1-32). Jacques Derrida spoke out for a critical reading of Schmitt with reference to the present international situation ('Autoimmunity: Real and Symbolic Suicides: A Dialogue with Jacques Derrida'). Georges Corm thinks that 'the deviations which we have witnessed since the grave events of 11 September 2001 and the energy used by the United States to impress on all minds the necessity of a total war on the terrorist monster' only confirm the 'penetrating views' of Carl Schmitt (*Orient-Occident: La fracture imaginaire,* 2nd ed. [Paris: Découverte, 2005], p. 194).

117 *Theorie des Partisanen. Zwischenbemerkung zum Begriff des Politischen* (Berlin: Duncker & Humblot, 1963), latest edition: Berlin 2002 (French translation: in *La notion de politique: Théorie du partisan* (Paris: Calmann-Lévy, 1972; 2nd ed.: Paris: Flammarion, 1992). Schmitt's book combines the text of the two speeches made in Spain in March 1962, some months after the construction of the Berlin Wall. Several commentators think that it is not accidental that it was at this moment of the Cold War that Schmitt's focus on this subject was crystallised. Carl Schmitt subsequently developed his views on the partisan in his interviews with the Maoist Joachim Schickel: *Gespräche mit Carl Schmitt* (Berlin: Merve, 1993). Cf. also Marcus Llanque, 'Ein Träger des Politischen nach dem Ende der Staatlichkeit: Der Partisan in Carl Schmitts politischer Theorie,' in Herfried Münkler (ed.), *Der Partisan: Theorie, Strategie, Gestalt* (Opladen: Westdeutscher, 1990), pp. 61-80; Joachim Klaus Ronneberger, 'Der Partisan im terroristischen Zeitalter: Vom gehegten Kriegsraum zum reinen Krieg, Carl Schmitt und Paul Virilio im Vergleich,' ibid., pp. 81-97 ; Ingeborg Villinger, 'Skalpell und Breitschwert: Im globalen Partisanentum droht der Ausnahmezustand zum Dauerzustand zu werden,' in *Frankfurter Allgemeine Zeitung,* 1. October 2001, p. 53; Teodoro Klitsche de La Grange, 'The Theory of the Partisan Today,' in *Telos* 127, Spring 2004, pp. 169-175; Douglas Bulloch, 'Carl Schmitt and the Theory of the Partisan: Articulating the Partisan in International Relations,' paper at the colloquium 'The International Thought of Carl Schmitt,' The Hague, 9-11 September 2004; Stephan Schlak, 'Der Partisan ganz privat,' in *Die Tageszeitung,* 15 March 2006, p. 15; and Matthias Schmoeckel, 'Carl Schmitts Begriff des Partisanen. Fragen zur Rechtsgeschichte des Partisanen und Terroristen,' in *Forum Historiae Iuris* [electronic journal], 31 March 2006, p. 29. One will note, finally, the appearance of a special issue of *CR: The New Centennial Review* entirely devoted to the examination of the theses of Carl Schmitt relative to the partisan: Michaelsen & David E. Johnson (eds.), *Theory of the Partisan,* East Lansing, Michigan State University Press, IV, 3, Winter 2004 (texts by Alfred Clement Goodson, Rodolphe

But it is first of all important to recall that, originally, the word 'terror' did not designate the action of the irregular partisan. 'Terror' was the generic name of the period extending from September 1793 to July 1794, during which the French Revolutionary forces made 'terror the order of the day' in order to suppress their political opponents. When he appears on the political scene, the 'terrorist' is thus not an irregular fighter who opposes the legitimacy of his action to the legality he is combating. On the contrary, he acted in accordance with the law. The 'Terror' of 1793 was a state phenomenon which coincided with one of the episodes of the French Revolution. It was exercised in the name of the state and, as such, supposes the legal monopoly on violence. The word 'terrorism' itself appears for the first time in the French language in 1794 to designate the regime of political 'terror' that then held sway. Two years later, it appeared in dictionaries. 'Millions of devils of hell called terrorists have been let loose on the world,' observed Edmund Burke at the time. The word thus originally referred to actions by a state or a political regime, that is, to legal actions (which one may consider illegitimate), and not to illegal actions (which could be considered legitimate). It is only later, in the course of the nineteenth century, that 'terrorism' would be perceived above all as an illegal form of action conducted against a state or political regime. It would then become loaded with negative connotations and cease to be used for designating one's own actions. (Although the word 'terror' would continue to be used to qualify certain measures adopted by totalitarian regimes, such as the Nazi regime or the Stalinist regime. One would then speak of 'terror,' but not of 'terrorism.' By this time, the two terms had been distinguished. This remark is important, for it allows us to understand how a concept such as state terrorism could, and can, exist.)

It is equally interesting to note that the appearance of the 'Terror' in France goes hand in hand with the implementation by the French revolutionaries, from April 1792, of the first war in history that one could qualify as a 'total war' — an expression which has never been applied, for example, to the religious wars of the sixteenth century nor to the Thirty Years' War, in spite of the numerous atrocities that were

Gasché, Gil Anidjar, Alberto Moreiras, Sigrid Weigel, Eva Horn, Miguel E. Vatter and Werner Hamacher).

committed especially in the latter of these conflicts.[118] Total war, as we have seen, is characterised notably by the abolition of traditional distinctions between civilians and combatants. In 1792, one of the driving forces of this novelty was the first real mass conscription in history, which created for the first time regiments entirely composed of freshly mobilised civilians ('regimentations' of masculine populations which, subsequently, would serve as a model for the control of civilian society by totalitarian regimes). A total war also immediately assigns to itself unlimited objectives and extends to all aspects of life in society. While the revolutionary 'terrorist' presented himself as undertaking a virtuous work (he 'purifies' the society), the revolutionary war affected both combatants and non-combatants. Those who conducted it themselves spoke of 'all-out war.' Jean-Baptise-Noël Bouchotte, Minister of War, emphasised the necessity of 'carrying the terror to our enemies.'[119] Robespierre called for the 'annihilation, extermination, and absolute destruction of the enemy.'[120] The same objective was applied to internal enemies, meaning that the external war and the civil war followed the same principles: during the War in the Vendée, the republican troops received explicit orders to take no prisoners and to massacre men, women and children without distinction. Total war, writes Jean-Yves Guiomar, 'is that which sets into motion masses of combatants never seen before, animated by the will to vanquish to the point of completely destroying the enemy. It is thus a war where no quarter is given, which rejects negotiation aimed at eliminating armed confrontation and bringing it to an end as quickly as possible.'[121] It represents a complete break with the principles of the 'regulated war' which prevailed before the Revolution.[122]

This unlimited war presents another remarkable characteristic: it is conducted in the name of 'freedom.' The revolutionaries who, in May 1790, had solemnly proclaimed their intention of 'forever'

118 Cf., for example, J. F. C. Fuller, *The Conduct of War, 1789-1961: A Study of the Impact of the French, Industrial, and Russian Revolution on War and Its Conduct*, p. 37.

119 Cited by Marcel Reinhard, *L'armée et la Révolution pendant la Convention* (Paris: Centre de documentation universitaire, 1957), p. 141.

120 Cited by Marcel Reinhard, in *Le Grand Carnot* (Paris: Hachette, 1994), p. 432.

121 Jean-Yves Guiomar, *L'invention de la guerre totale, XVIIIe-XXe siècle* (Paris: Félin, 2004), pp. 13-14.

122 Cf. André Corvisier (ed.), *De la guerre réglée à la guerre totale* (Paris: CTHS, 1997), 2 vols.

renouncing wars of conquest, justified their own action — and its unlimited character — by their intention of 'delivering oppressed peoples,' of fighting all monarchical power and of spreading the principles of the Revolution throughout the world. If they attacked neighbouring countries, it was to 'export freedom'; if they committed massacres, it was because a goal so morally (and ideologically) elevated justified the implementation of any means. The relation between moral war and total war, well highlighted by Carl Schmitt, finds here a new and striking illustration.[123]

For Carl Schmitt, the figure of the partisan is quite essential, for it constitutes a perfect demonstration that the state and politics are not necessarily synonymous, but can, on the contrary, be disconnected. The partisan in fact conducts an eminently political struggle, but one which is undertaken outside the control of the state, and even generally directed against the state. The actions of partisans show that there are wars other than those between states and enemies who are not states.

Schmitt distinguishes between the figure of the *partisan*, as he appeared in the guerrilla warfare against Napoleonic occupation in Prussia and Spain at the beginning of the nineteenth century, and the modern *revolutionary combatant*.[124] Both are of course irregular combatants who act outside the current legal order and who oppose to this legality a legitimacy to which they appeal and that they claim they embody. Both are 'irregulars' who describe themselves as 'resistance fighters' while they are concomitantly stigmatised not only as 'illegal' combatants but also as 'illegitimate' combatants by the official powers who deny them the right to resist and rebel. Both (and Schmitt focuses especially on this point) have a sharp awareness of the friend and of the enemy, since they do not need to have an enemy designated in order to fight him (just as the terrorist considers as an enemy person whom no public or legal authority presents to him as such). Both, finally, shatter through their very acts the traditional distinction between civilians and soldiers which originally converged with that

---

123 Jean-Yves Guiomar himself emphasises in his book that 'the analysis presented by Carl Schmitt has great strength' (*L'invention de la guerre totale*, p. 313).

124 Schmitt cites, besides, a Prussian general, according to whom the campaign conducted by Napoleon against Prussia in 1806 could itself be considered as a partisan war on a grand scale. Cf. Ernesto Laclau, 'On "Real" and "Absolute" Enemies,' in *CR: The New Centennial Review*, Spring 2005, pp. 1-12.

of the combatant and the non-combatant (the civilian was considered as not taking part in war, for which reason he enjoyed special protection). Partisans, in fact, are not necessarily soldiers; they are rarely that. They are most often civilians who have decided to take up arms. And these civilians themselves often attack other civilians whom they consider as accomplices or allies of their enemies.

Partisans and revolutionary combatants, for all that, differ deeply from one another. To the partisan, apart from the irregularity and the intensity of his political engagement, Carl Schmitt attributes as a distinguishing criterion flexibility and mobility in active combat, but above all his telluric (*tellurisch*)[125] character. The partisan's objectives are generally limited and related to his own territory. Whether he wishes to put an end to a foreign occupation or topple a political regime which he judges illegitimate, his actions are related to a particular territory. His actions, therefore, come under the logic of the Earth.

Not so the 'combatant of the revolution' or the 'revolutionary activist,' whose appearance Carl Schmitt traces back to Lenin,[126] who identifies himself with 'the absolute aggressiveness of an ideology' or claims to embody the ideal of an 'abstract justice.' It may originally have been a partisan of the classical type who 'is drawn into the force field of irresistible technical-industrial progress.'[127] 'His mobility is so enhanced by motorization that he runs the risk of complete dislocation. [...] A motorized partisan loses his *tellurian* character.'[128] The loss of his territorial character comes from the fact that the revolutionary combatant is not linked in an intrinsic manner to a single territory: virtually, the entire planet constitutes his field of action. But the lack of limitation operates on him also on another level. The 'revolutionary combatant' is freed from all limits in the choice of means. Convinced

---

125 Meaning territorial, from the Latin *tellus*, which means earth or land.-Ed.

126 In the *Nouvelle Gazette rhénane* of 7 November 1848, Karl Marx already cited 'revolutionary terrorism' as one of the means to be used to obtain victory. But it was Lenin who would make violence the unavoidable point of departure of power for the proletariat. With the advent of the Russia of the Soviets, the word 'terror' would besides find for some time a certain favour. Reentering the Soviet Union, the communists Cachin and Frossard indicated that they had adopted the 'methods of violence and terror to which a class that aspires to gain power is inevitably obliged to resort' (*L'Humanité*, 3 August 1920).

127 *The Theory of the Partisan*, p. 14.

128 *The Theory of the Partisan*, p. 14.

as he is that he is waging an absolutely 'just' war, he is radicalised in a sense at once ideological and moral. He invariably designates his enemy as a criminal and, in turn, he is himself designated as such. With the revolutionary combatant comes absolute hostility. For Lenin, writes Carl Schmitt, 'The purpose is the communist revolution in all countries of the world; whatever serves this purpose is good and just. [...] Only revolutionary war is true war for Lenin, because it derives from absolute enmity. [...] With the ascension of the party to absolute status, the partisan too became absolute, elevated to the status of the bearer of absolute enmity.'[129]

'Where war is conducted on both sides as an undiscriminating war,' adds Schmitt, '[...] the partisan is a marginal figure who does not break out of the framework of war, and who changes nothing in the larger structure of the political process. Only when the war opponents are criminalized as such, when war is conducted as in civil war as a class struggle, or when its main goal is the elimination of the government of the enemy state, then the criminalizing of the enemy represents a revolutionary blast that works in such a way as to make the partisan the real hero of the war. For it is he who applies the death sentence against the criminal, and risks being considered himself a criminal or pest. Such is the logic of a war of *justa causa* [just cause] in the absence of recognition of a *justa hostis* [just enemy].'[130] The terrorist of today is evidently the heir to, or the latest incarnation of, this figure.

To what degree do these two types of partisans overlap with the corsair and pirate, respectively? Julien Freund wrote twenty years ago that 'partisan war and present-day terrorism are in some way the reproduction on land of the corsair and the pirate [...]. The present-day figure of the partisan is, so to speak, the ground-based replica of the corsair, that of the terrorist the replica of the pirate. Doubtless there is a logical connection even in the irregularity, in the sense that it was sometimes difficult to trace a limit between the corsair and the pirate; it is the same in the case of the partisan and the terrorist.'[131] Schmitt in fact sees in the figure of the corsair the predecessor of the partisan. He speaks of the corsair who enjoys public recognition even though

---

129 *The Theory of the Partisan*, p. 35 & 66.

130 *The Theory of the Partisan*, p. 21.

131 Afterword to Carl Schmitt, *Terre et Mer: Un point de vue sur l'histoire mondiale* (Paris: Labyrinthe, 1985), pp. 108-109.

he acts in an irregular manner, in contrast to the pirate who is considered a criminal and is recognised by nobody. However, the corsair acts on the sea, whereas the partisan, for Schmitt, is essentially tied to the land. As for the modern terrorist, he transcends all these distinctions. He is evidently not comparable to the corsair, but he is not comparable to the pirate either, for his motivations, which are eminently political, are unrelated to self-interest or profit. Besides, he acts also in space, that is, beyond Earth and Sea.

Schmitt rejects the idea that technological and industrial progress is going to render the figure of the partisan obsolete. He contends, on the contrary, with a remarkable lucidity, that this very progress is going to add a new dimension to the partisan. 'But what if,' he wonders, 'the human type that went into the partisan adapted to its new technical-industrial environment, learned how to make use of the new means, and developed a new, adapted form of the partisan? [...] Who can prevent [...] unanticipated new sorts of enmity come into being, whose realization evokes unanticipated forms of appearances/ apparitions of a new partisanship?'[132] Schmitt heralds here, in a prophetic manner, the era of the 'global partisan' (*Kosmopartisan*).

Terrorism is today obviously no longer a new phenomenon.[133] What is new is the central place that it occupies (or that is attributed to

---

132 *The Theory of the Partisan*, pp. 56 & 168.

133 David C. Rapoport, professor at the University of California at Los Angeles and founder of the journal *Terrorism and Political Violence*, distinguishes four great waves of terrorism in modern history. The first, which begins in Russia in the 1880s and spread rapidly into the Balkans and Western Europe, was mostly the work of anarchists. The passage from the nineteenth to the twentieth century would be 'the golden age of the political assassination.' These first terrorist actions of the modern age are associated with the development of the daily press, the rise of modern means of transport and the invention of the telegraph (cf. 'Terrorisme et médiatisme,' in *De defensa*, 25 May 1998, pp. 16-19). The second wave is the anticolonialist wave, which began around 1920 and continued for some forty years, culminating around the sixties. It is this which would give credence to the idea that the terrorists are above all 'freedom fighters.' The third wave, of a smaller scope, is that of the ultra-Leftist organisations which, after the death of 'Che' Guevara, preach urban guerrilla warfare: the Red Brigades (Italy), Action directe (France), the Red Army Faction (Germany), but also Tupamaros (Uruguay), Montoneros (Argentina), etc. This wave, which has today receded in the majority of Western countries, survives still in Nepal, Peru, Colombia, etc. The last is the present wave of a global, predominantly 'Islamist' terrorism. It sees the generalisation of suicide attacks, very inappropriately called 'kamikazes' (since the Japanese kamikazes of the Second World War were perfectly regular soldiers who, moreover, never aimed at civilian targets), without however having invented them (in the nineteenth century, the one who carried out an attack using dynamite was also frequently killed by his own

it) nowadays on the international scene. But here one is struck by the contrast between the omnipresent denunciations of 'terrorism' and the semantic vagueness of the concept, a vagueness which makes it easier to exploit the term.

One of the first questions to arise has to do with the idea of the legitimacy of terrorist actions, a legitimacy constantly claimed by terrorists but denied by their adversaries. The problem of the partisan calls for a questioning of the terms 'legality' and 'legitimacy.' Because he is an illegal combatant, the partisan can only claim a legitimacy superior to the positive law decreed by the authority he combats, which amounts to disputing whether legality and legitimacy could ever merge. That is another Schmittian theme par excellence.[134]

It is undeniable that certain forms of 'terrorism' have been recognised as legitimate in recent times, for example, the forces resisting German occupation during the Second World War (although these were invariably characterised as 'terrorists' by the German occupying forces), and also the numerous groups who fought for independence from the old colonial powers, presenting themselves as 'freedom

---

bomb). Certain authors date this wave to the summer of 1968, the date when the Popular Front for the Liberation of Palestine (PFLP) of George Habash hijacked two planes of the Israeli company 'El Al.' However, one still cannot still speak at that time of 'global terrorism.' The year 1979, on the other hand, marked an essential turning point since it saw (besides the beginning of a new century of the Islamic era) both the Iranian Revolution and the invasion of Afghanistan by the Soviets. The Islamic Revolution of Tehran was essentially anti-American, but the United States did not hesitate to support and finance the Islamic Afghan militants, whose resistance was to end ten years later, in 1989, with the retreat of the Red Army. After the fall of the Berlin Wall and the dismantling of the Soviet system, certain Islamist combatants trained in Afghanistan continued their battle in Algeria and in the former Soviet republics with a strong Muslim population (Chechnya, Uzbekistan, Kyrgyzstan, Tajikistan, Azerbaijan, etc.), then in Iraq and elsewhere. At the time of the Cold War, the terrorist groups were frequently thought of as being manipulated by the Soviet KGB. The disappearance of the KGB has, however, not made terrorism decrease, quite the contrary. On the history of terrorism, cf. also Joachim Schickel, *Guerilleros, Partisanen: Theorie und Praxis* (Munich: Carl Hanser, 1970) (which gives a major place to the theses of Carl Schmitt); Walter Laqueur, *The Age of Terrorism* (Boston: Little Brown,1987; and Alex P. Schmid and Albert J. Jongman (eds.), *Political Terrorism: A New Guide to Actors, Authors, Concepts, Theories, Data Bases, and Literature* (New Brunswick: Transaction Books, 1988).

134 Cf. Carl Schmitt, *Legalität und Legitimität* (Munich-Leipzig: Duncker & Humblot, 1932), latest edition: Berlin 2006; French translation: *Légalité — légitimité* (Paris: Librairie générale de droit et de jurisprudence, 1936), 2nd ed.: 'Légalité et légitimité,' in Carl Schmitt, *Du politique: 'Légalité et légitimité' et autres essais* (Puiseaux: Pardès,1990), pp. 39-79; English translation: *Legality and Legitimacy* (Durham: Duke University Press, 2004).

fighters.' The four Geneva Conventions of 12 August 1949, for example, grant resistance fighters most of the rights and privileges enjoyed
by regular combatants.[135] After 1945, in the epoch of the anticolonial
struggles, innumerable armed minorities, 'liberation movements' and
guerrillas represented themselves as resistance fighters, while governments characterised them as 'subversive groups' and 'terrorists.'
When their struggles ended and they had obtained a certain degree of
international recognition, the means employed by them in retrospect
appeared legitimate. The idea that in certain cases terrorism could
be legitimate thus took hold. Of course, it was also claimed that terrorism could not be justified when the political and social objectives
could be achieved by other means. But opinions were bound to differ in respect of the criteria for distinguishing 'good' terrorism from
'bad.' The appreciation of the moral or immoral character of terrorism
was thus bound to come under the heading of propaganda or mere
subjectivity.[136]

The distinction between 'resistance organisations' and 'terrorists'
becomes even more vague due to the fact that certain countries owe
their birth or their independence partly to terrorism, and that certain
events or regime changes have brought former terrorists to power,
transforming them by the same stroke into respected representatives
of their countries, or at least parties that can be negotiated with. The
former terrorists Menachem Begin and Yitzhak Shamir, who were
known for carrying out attacks against Arab civilians before the state
of Israel was proclaimed, subsequently rose to the highest offices of
their country.[137] The same goes for the Algerian and South African
leaders Ahmed Ben Bella and Nelson Mandela.

Even today, one man's 'freedom fighter' is another man's 'terrorist.' The usage of the term is arbitrary and can even be reversed. Even

---

135 It must, however, be noted that, in theory, guerrilla fighters, though irregular
combatants, are themselves considered to be bearing their arms in a visible manner
and possessing distinctive signs which normally oblige the states to treat them as
soldiers.

136 The expression 'freedom fighter,' very much in vogue at the time of the anticolonial
battles, began to fall out of use only quite recently. It is only in the course of the
1970s that the UN organised its first international conferences 'with a view to
suppressing terrorist attacks.'

137 The Jewish terrorist group Irgun led by Menachem Begin was the first to describe
themselves as 'freedom fighters' fighting against 'government terror,' contrary to the
contemporary Lehi group (the Stern Gang), which claimed the label of 'terrorist.'

as it supported Islamist movements in order to balance the influence of secular Arab nationalist movements, the United States, during the epoch of the Cold War, never hesitated to support certain terrorist groups, notably in Nicaragua, Angola and Afghanistan — just as it supported, after the first Gulf War, Iraqi opposition groups responsible for numerous car bombings.[138] The same Taliban that was described as 'freedom fighters' during the Soviet occupation of Afghanistan instantly became 'terrorists' when they began using the same methods against their former allies. The militants of the KLA, presented as 'resistance fighters' when NATO forces bombed Serbia, became 'terrorists' when they attacked NATO's ally Macedonia. Many such examples can be produced.[139]

The illegality of terrorism must, besides, be placed within the more general context of a de-institutionalisation of political life in numerous countries and the rapid expansion of uncontrolled areas ('grey areas') in the world: the proliferation of urban jungles in the large megapolises in the global south, drug traffic on a global scale, formation of veritable private armies in the service of organised crime, the appearance of 'cyberguerillas' able to unleash artificial stock crashes, the blurring of the boundary between financial and criminal activities, and so on.[140]

The question of the status of terrorism in relation to the legality-legitimacy distinction is finally complicated by the existence of 'legal' terrorism in the form of terrorism resorted to by states. The most current definitions of terrorism do not exclude state terrorism which,

---

138 Cf. Patrick Cockburn, 'Clinton Backed Baghdad Bombers' in *The Independent*, 26 March 1996; and Alain Gresh, 'Croisade antiterroriste,' in *Le Monde diplomatique*, September 1996.

139 The disagreement between Americans and Europeans on the subject of the characterisation applicable to movements like the Palestinian Hamas or the Lebanese Hezbollah is another illustration of the difficulty of establishing a clear-cut border between 'resistance' and 'terrorism.' According to Israeli law, the violent actions committed by the Palestinians are crimes or offences whose authors cannot benefit from the law applying to prisoners of war. But, at the same time, the reprisal actions conducted against them are officially characterised as acts of war, which therefore do not come within the scope of reparations in cases of damages caused to third parties, and not as police acts, which, in the case of such damages, could entitle reparations. Cf., on this subject, Henry Laurens, 'La poudrière proche-orientale entre terrorisme classique et violence graduée du Hezbollah,' in *Esprit*, May 2005, pp. 141-149.

140 The trans-national politico-criminal organisations apparently handle almost $70 billion each year, and recycle half of it back into the world economy.

it should be emphasised, is responsible for more deaths than illegal, non-state terrorism.[141] If, in fact, one defines terrorism as a way of causing the greatest possible damage to the greatest possible number of innocent victims, as a way of deliberately killing innocents chosen randomly in order to demoralise a population, or to force political leaders to capitulate, then there is no doubt that the terror bombings of civilian German and Japanese populations during the Second World War fits into this category since civilians were deliberately targeted.

The question of whether the so-called 'hyper-terrorism' or 'global terrorism' of today only represents an amplification of the most characteristic elements of 'classical' terrorism, or if it signifies the emergence of a truly new form of violence is frequently discussed today. Let us therefore briefly consider certain traits of this 'new' terrorism.

One of the first characteristics of contemporary global terrorism is its lack of limitations, one of the hallmarks of the revolutionary combatant. Terrorism always includes violence, but violence does not suffice to define it. It is necessary to consider the type of violence which is used. Global terrorism is always engaged in a struggle to the death and recognises no limits to the exercise of violence. The terrorists consider the classic distinctions between belligerents and neutrals, civilians and soldiers, combatants or non-combatants, legitimate or illegitimate targets, to be irrelevant. In this respect terrorism resembles total war. The mirror image of this form of unlimited action is the risk that any means may be considered to be justified in the struggle against terrorism. 'One must operate as a partisan everywhere where there are partisans,' said Napoleon already in 1813. Terrorism being posited as an absolute enemy, it is tempting to think that no means can be *a priori* excluded in order to put an end to it — especially if one believes that the classical (or democratic) means are ineffective when facing such a threat. The use of torture, for example, has been legitimated several times by the necessities of the war on terror (to obtain information, for example, or to prevent terrorist attacks). The temptation to fight the terrorists with their own means is considerable.

Another important characteristic is an even more pronounced deterritorialisation. In the postmodern epoch, that of the end of territorial logic, the figure of the partisan, to whom Carl Schmitt still attributed a marked 'telluric' character, is becoming deterritorialised.

---

141 Cf. Gérard Chaliand, 'La mesure du terrorisme,' in *Stratégique*, 1997, 2-3, p. 10.

The war against terrorism no longer has any territorial foundations. The enemy is not (or only to a small degree) identified with a particular territory. Paul Virilio has gone so far as to speak of 'the end of geography,' which is no doubt excessive, for the facts of geopolitics remain. Nonetheless, the preferred form of terrorist groups today is the *network*. What one calls 'Al Qaeda,' for example, is not an organisation in the traditional sense, located in a particular place and with a clear hierarchy, but a vague conglomerate of tangled networks. These terrorist networks take on all the more importance in that the postmodern epoch is itself, above all, an epoch of networks, an epoch where the transverse networks are displacing pyramidal organisations. And these networks are scattered: their members live in many countries, which accentuates their de-territorialisation. Moreover, if the partisan is becoming increasingly less 'telluric,' it is because the territorial form of domination itself is becoming obsolete: it is more profitable nowadays to colonise minds or to control markets than to conquer or annex territories.

In this respect, the parallels that have often been drawn between the attacks of 11 September and the attack on Pearl Harbor in 1941, by George W. Bush among others,[142] are deceptive. The attack of 1941 was the act of a country clearly locatable on the map: Japan. The attacks of September 11 were carried out by international networks. The United States was of course able to go to war with Afghanistan, which was accused of serving as a refuge or 'sanctuary' for Al Qaeda groups, but these groups were only partially and provisionally domiciled or accommodated there. The 'global' war launched by the United States against terrorism thus pits, on the one side, 'partisans' without a precise territorial connection, being essentially organised in networks, and on the other side a power which aspires no longer to conquer territories but to establish a new world order perceived as a necessary condition of its national security, this new world order implying the global opening of markets, guaranteed access to energy resources, the suppression of regulations and borders, the control of communications, and so on. Under such conditions it is no longer the logic of territory that characterises the action of the partisans but the 'maritime' logic of deterritorialisation/globalisation which favours

---

142 According to Bob Woodward, George W. Bush described the attacks of 11 September in his personal diary as 'the Pearl Harbor of the 21st century' (cf. Bob Woodward, *Plan of Attack* [New York: Simon & Schuster, 2004], p. 41).

the emergence of a new form of terrorism, as it opens up new means of action to it.[143] And, since the United States, as Carl Schmitt defines it, itself represents maritime power par excellence, and globalisation also obeys a form of 'maritime' logic, one can say that the war against terrorism itself is governed entirely by maritime logic.

The appearance of an entirely deterritorialised terrorism has another consequence. It brings about the conflation of military and police operations of which we have spoken earlier. During the Second World War, in order to combat the Resistance, the occupation forces had to engage in typical police work (conducting searches, arresting and interrogating suspects, etc.) whereas one could simultaneously discern a militarisation of the police called upon to collaborate with them. Similarly, during the anticolonial wars, the regular forces gradually began to use police methods, since their task was first of all to identify an enemy that did not wear a uniform. In the war against global terrorism, this conflation of the roles of the police and the army have reached such proportions that it shatters the distinction between internal affairs and international affairs.[144]

Terrorism, finally, constitutes war in times of peace, and is therefore also in this respect emblematic of a growing lack of distinction between these two concepts. But this war, as we have just said, resembles above all a police action. Now, a policeman does not consider his adversaries as a 'traditional' soldier considers his. By definition, the police are not content merely to fight crime. They seek to eradicate it. They cannot negotiate or conclude a 'peace treaty' with criminals. In this respect, there is nothing political in the activities of the police, at

---

143 On the link between terrorism and globalisation, and the gap that the latter creates between the countries connected to a globalised 'centre' functioning as a core and the others, cf., notably, Thomas P. M. Barnett, *The Pentagon's New Map: War and Peace in the Twenty-first Century* (New York: Putnam, 2004).

144 From 2000, the 'blending' of systems of internal security and military strategies has been presented in the United States as the ideal global framework of the fight against terrorist threats (cf. Carolyn Pumphrey, ed., *Transnational Threats: Blending Law Enforcement and Military Strategies* [U.S. Army War College, November 2000]). The 2002 report entitled *The National Security Strategy of the United States* itself confirms that '[t]oday, the distinction between domestic and foreign affairs is diminishing' (p. 31). The specialists on the war against terrorism for their part increase their appeals to the advice of criminologists (cf. Xavier Raufer, 'Géopolitique et criminology: Une féconde alliance face aux dangers du monde,' in *Défense nationale et sécurité collective*, May 2005). On the concept of an international police ('Globo-Cop'), cf. Alessandro Dal Lago, *Polizia globale: Guerra e conflitti dopo l'11 settembre* (Verona: Ombre corta, 2003).

least not when they engage their traditional adversaries, criminals and delinquents. On the other hand there is an obviously 'moral' dimension: crime is blameworthy not only socially, but also morally. In this regard, the 'police' character of the war against terror is revealing. It underlies, as Rik Coolsaet writes, this '19th-century principle [which continues to exist today] that terrorism is not a legitimate political activity but a criminal offence.'[145] But what exactly is it? Is terrorism a new political form of war or a new type of crime?[146]

For those who combat terrorism everything is clear. In the public discourse that they employ to characterise their adversaries, the terrorists are invariably described as criminals. This phenomenon is not new, either. Under the Revolution, the Vendée insurgents were officially designated 'brigands.' After the assassination in September 1901 of the American President William McKinley by an anarchist, his successor Theodore Roosevelt described the anarchists as 'criminals against the human race.'[147] But the equation: terrorists = criminals, based in general on the violent, blind and unpredictable character of the actions committed by the terrorists, has also been employed in the past to characterise the members of the Resistance or the 'freedom fighters' of the anticolonial struggles. By that reasoning, it became possible to treat them as simple criminals, which justified, for example, the refusal to give them the status of political prisoners. The terrorist, Pierre Mannoni writes, is regularly described in terms such as 'criminal,' 'assassin,' or 'bandit,' reducing him to the rank of undesirable violent persons, disturbers of the peace and of the social

---

145 Rik Coolsaet, Al-Qaeda — The Myth: The Root Causes of International Terrorism and How to Tackle Them (Gent: Academia Press, 2005), p. 59.

146 On this point, cf. Christopher Daase, 'Terrorismus und Krieg: Zukunftsszenarien politischer Gewalt nach dem 11. September 2001,' in Rüdiger Voigt (ed.), Krieg: Instrument der Politik? Bewaffnete Konflikte im Übergang vom 20. zum 21. Jahrhundert (Baden-Baden: Nomos, 2002), pp. 365-389. Cf. also Richard Falk, 'Thinking About Terrorism,' in The Nation, 28 June 1986; Teodoro Klitsche de la Grange, 'Osservazioni sul terrorismo post-moderno,' in Behemoth 30, 2001; and Jörg Friedrichs, 'Defining the International Public Enemy: The Political Struggle behind the Legal Debate on International Terrorism,' in Leiden Journal of International Law XIX, 2006, 1, pp. 69-91.

147 More than a decade later, the public prosecutor of Woodrow Wilson passed a bill aiming at expelling all anarchists by ship, regardless of the uncertainty of their eventual involvement in a criminal type of action. This decision provoked a bomb attack against Wall Street in 1920, following which the American authorities adopted a very restrictive law on the immigration quotas related to citizens of Eastern and Central Europe.

order, or as 'barbaric,' 'wild,' or 'mad,' ascribing to him mental ill-
ness or a brutal, uncivilised nature.[148] According to Michael Walzer
'terrorists evoke those unchained killers who slaughter everything in
their path.'[149] Terrorists would thus be either criminals or madmen.

Such denunciations depict the terrorist as an enemy who has nothing whatsoever in common with those who fight against him. The
terrorist becomes the Other, a *hostis humani generis.*'[150] 'The image
of the other that is conveyed is of one who will never be able 'to be
like us.'[151] In the media and in political discourse it is constantly
proclaimed that the causes championed by terrorists are 'incomprehensible.' This inability to comprehend is particularly widespread in
the United States, since Americans, convinced of having created the
best possible society — nay, the only truly acceptable one — have quite
naturally a tendency to find it unimaginable that someone may reject
the model they champion. The idea that America is the land of the
free, the ultimate model of how societies should be organised, and
at the same time the nation chosen by Providence, makes it easier to
represent terrorists as sick people, perverts or madmen: in September
2001, how could 'normal' people not believe in the 'goodness' of the
American people? 'How could people who had the least of everything
that counts think that those who had the most of it owed it to anything
but their merit?'[152] The sole fact that the terrorists 'hate the United
States and everything for which it stands'[153] already makes them
exceptional beings — and, as America is identified with good, makes
them incarnations of evil. This being so, terrorism can be stigmatised
as at the same time irrational and criminal, devoid of all logic, and
fundamentally without a properly political objective.

This description of the terrorist, either as a madman, a criminal,
or, more often still, as a criminal madman, undoubtedly resonates
with public opinion, which often considers the terrorist acts as at once

---

148 Pierre Mannoni, *Les logiques du terrorisme* (Paris: In Press, 2004), p. 41. After the
    attacks of 7 July 2005 in London, the BBC had advised its journalists not to speak
    any longer of 'terrorists,' but of 'bombers.'

149 Michael Walzer, *De la guerre et du terrorisme*, p. 80.

150 Latin: 'enemy of mankind.'-Ed.

151 Francesco Ragazzi, 'The National Security Strategy of the USA ou la rencontre
    improbable de Grotius, Carl Schmitt et Philip K. Dick.'

152 Immanuel Wallenstein, *Sortir du monde états-unien* (Paris: Liana Levi, 2004), p. 66.

153 *The National Security Strategy of the United States*, p. 14.

unjustifiable and incomprehensible ('why do they do it?' 'what *do* they want?'). These reactions can themselves be perfectly understood. But the question is if the recourse to such terms does not prevent the analysis of the true nature of terrorism and, further, the identification of its causes.

The description of the terrorist as a simple 'criminal' is based on the argument that forbids any reconciliation between killing and legitimacy. This argument however comes up against the fact that, in every war, killing is legitimate — even when it is a question of civilians, victims of terror bombings or of 'collateral damages.' Terrorists thus strive, in their rhetoric, to include their actions within the sphere of legitimate violence. In fact, every terrorist considers, as we have seen, that he is in effect fighting a war, and that his action is perfectly legitimate. The violence exercised by him, he claims, is only the consequence or the mirror image of the other side's 'legal' use of force, and constitutes a reaction that is justified by the injustice of the situation.

In opposition to this rhetoric, which is denounced as specious, the terrorist's enemies describe him as a criminal whom one only reluctantly admits could have political aims. It is argued that his methods disqualify him from presenting himself as a political combatant. Based on these methods, he is rejected as a criminal. But the denial of the political character of terrorism is not explained only by the emotional reactions of public opinion. On the part of the public authorities, it often expresses an eminently political attitude based on these emotional reactions. 'It smacks of a deliberate will to compromise the political message inherent in the terrorist act,' writes Percy Kemp, 'as it smacks of a denial of truth understood as a condition *sine qua non* of the constitution of a new ethos. Thus, in Israel, the refusal of the authorities to recognise the specifically political character of terrorism (and thus their refusal of any negotiation) finds its bases in the denial of the truth of the plunder of the Palestinians. In the United States, such a refusal is based on the official denial of the reality of the incestuous relations that the successive administrations have undertaken with the Islamic movement and the subsequent desertion of these cumbersome allies at the end of the Cold War.'[154]

At the same time, it is admitted that the terrorists are fighting a war against the United States and that the U.S. must therefore make

---

154 Percy Kemp, 'Terroristes, ou anges vengeurs,' in *Esprit*, May 2004, pp. 21-22.

war on them. But the use of the term 'war' is ambiguous. Traditional wars are concluded by peace treaties, which is not an option in this case. This type of war thus resembles a total, moral or 'police' war, where the objective is not only to defeat the enemy but to wipe him out. Carl Schmitt writes that 'theologians tend to define the enemy as something that should be annihilated.'[155] This is also how the advocates of the 'just war' and those who prosecute the 'war on terror' reason, thereby justifying the goal of not just fighting terrorism, but making it disappear. This type of war is by its nature very different from traditional wars, in that it is similar both to police actions and to total war.[156]

One does not negotiate with terrorists: this is what all public authorities who are confronted with it always say (even if, in reality, they do sometimes engage in more or less covert negotiations, for example by discreetly offering a ransom to obtain the release of a hostage). Global terrorism also seems not to want to negotiate—which distinguishes it from kidnapping, which it otherwise resembles — but only to cause the greatest possible damage. However, if one admits that the true target of global terrorism is never that which the actual terrorist acts are directed at, but that which it seeks to achieve by these acts (for example, to force a government to change its attitude or to modify its policies in certain respects), then one must also admit that the terrorists, on the contrary, in fact do seek a form of 'negotiation.'

---

155 *Ex captivitate salus* (Cologne: Greven, 1950), p. 89 (latest edition: Berlin: Duncker & Humblot, 2002; French translation: *Ex captivitate salus: Expériences des années 1945-1947* (Paris: J. Vrin, 2003).

156 Gilles Andréani, in a text entitled 'La guerre contre le terrorisme: Le piège des mots' (electronic document, 2004), also shows that, in the expression 'war on terrorism,' the word 'war' cannot be equivocal. He notes that the use of this word paradoxically amplifies the enemy whom one attacks and confers on him a certain legitimacy, but that it is radically contradicted by the treatment that one gives him when one has made him harmless, since he is not considered as a prisoner of war but as an 'illegal combatant' without a uniform, being part of neither a precise territory nor an organised command. Other doubts have been expressed by Michael Howard ('What's in a Name: How to Fight Terrorism,' in *Foreign Affairs*, January-February 2002). Michael Walzer remarks for his part, very correctly, that the 'war against terrorism' is above all 'a police work,' but that at the same time it makes use of military means, whereas the police, except in cases of legitimate defence, 'are not authorised to kill civilians, even if it is a question of criminals.' 'If you think about it,' he adds, 'the rules of police work concerning the collateral damages are much more restrictive than those that soldiers use' ('Terrorisme, morale et guerre juste,' interview with Jean-Marc Flükiger at www.terrorisme.net/p/article_206.shtml, 30 April 2006).

Terrorism seeks to obtain something: that France stop lending its support to the Algerian regime, that the United States change its policy in the Middle East, that Russia leave Chechnya, and so on. The statement that 'one does not negotiate with terrorism' is then to be understood as a simple refusal to yield to a demand. Of course, public authorities base their refusal to yield to such demands on the means employed by terrorists (which are considered to be unacceptable because 'innocent persons' are targeted or the civilian population is 'held hostage'). But it is quite obvious that they would not yield even if the same demands were presented to them in a 'reasonable' manner, and that is indeed why terrorists choose to use the most extreme means — means they consider may succeed in obtaining what they would not obtain otherwise, although they are on the contrary going to be used as a justification to reject the terrorists' demands.

Carl Schmitt distinguishes the traditional partisan from the 'absolute partisan' who, driven by his revolutionary faith, frees himself from all norms. Nevertheless, Schmitt does not consider the absolute partisan to be a criminal. On the contrary, he recognises in him an eminently political figure. He notes that '[t]he intensely political character of the partisan is crucial since he has to be distinguished from the common thief and criminal, whose motives aim at private enrichment.'[157] Even when it appears to be driven by nothing but self-interest, every terrorist act is in fact a bearer of a political message which should be deciphered. For the terrorist, terror is always potentially 'convertible into political capital' (Percy Kemp). The terrorist is indeed a *hostis*, a political enemy in Carl Schmitt's sense, but it is precisely this properly political dimension of terrorism that the recourse to crime-fighting rhetoric tends to erase. 'The more the democracies ignore the political message carried by terrorism,' adds Percy Kemp, 'the more they encourage an escalation of violence by inviting the terrorist to transform himself into an avenging angel.'[158] That does not mean that terrorist acts are not also crimes. But they are *political* crimes which cannot be recognised as such without taking into consideration the context and the causes which allow them to be qualified in this way. In other terms, a political crime is political

---

157 *The Theory of the Partisan*, p. 10.

158 Percy Kemp, 'Terroristes, ou anges vengeurs,' p. 20.

before being criminal, and that is why it cannot be equated with an 'ordinary' crime.

The limitations of the thesis according to which terrorism can be used only 'as a last resort,' that it is 'the weapon of the poor,' and expresses only the 'despair' of certain populations or minorities, have been easily pointed out by several authors. But the thesis according to which terrorist violence is 'illogical,' 'irrational,' 'inexplicable,' purely 'inhuman,' 'criminal' or 'barbaric' is even less tenable. There is nothing 'irrational' about terrorism. It is not more (or less) irrational than the logic of the market, which also has its religious foundations, since it divides the world into 'believers' (in the absolute power of the 'invisible hand' and spontaneous economic regulation) and 'unbelievers.' Let us add that it is erroneous to qualify Islamic terrorism as 'nihilist' insofar as nihilism is the *bête noire* of Islamic thought. (What the Muslims reproach the West most for is precisely its nihilism, which is related to the fact that it has only materialistic values to propose as a model.) Nothing is thus more removed from reality than the representation of terrorism as an irrational set of purely pathological or criminal actions. Terrorism falls within a political design, it responds to a strategic logic. This logic and this design are lost sight of by purely moral condemnations or the indignation of the media. 'Even the blind attacks,' writes Pierre Mannoni, 'affecting anonymous victims, are deliberately chosen and follow a precise intention. Everything in it is calculated to produce a certain type of effect, for nothing is less fantastic, vague or improvised than an attack where everything is planned: actors, places, modalities and, above all, media impact and political effects.'[159] 'All the indignation and moral condemnation,' he adds, 'finally and in spite of itself, only sanction the terrorism that they denounce by bearing witness to its capacity to rattle minds.'[160]

During the Cold War, the Soviet Union represented for America a 'symmetrical' enemy. With global terrorism, it is an asymmetrical confrontation. 'War,' observes Pierre Mannoni, 'admits a relation of direct proportionality between a wide spatial expansion, moderate-to-strong intensity and a constant frequency; terrorism is characterised by a relation of inverse proportionality between a weak spatial

---

159 *Les logiques du terrorisme*, p. 8.
160 *Les logiques du terrorisme*, p. 17.

expansion, extreme intensity and sporadic frequency.'[161] Formerly one sought the balance of powers (or of 'terror'). Henceforth the key concept is that of asymmetry (not dissymmetry, which designates only an inequality of a qualitative order between the powers that be). The 'war against terrorism' is by its very nature an asymmetric conflict: it is precisely because the terrorist does not have classic means of confrontation at his disposal that he has recourse to terrorism. This asymmetry existed already in the era of the classic partisan, which aroused Napoleon's anger. With global terrorism, this asymmetry is generalised at all levels. Asymmetry of the actors: on one side the heavy structures of the state, on the other a fluid approach and transnational groups.[162] Asymmetry of objectives: the terrorists know where and how they will strike, their adversaries do not know (or know only imperfectly) where and how to respond. Asymmetry of means: on 11 September 2001, for a few minutes, warships, atom bombs, F-16s and cruise missiles became obsolete in the face of 19 'fanatics' armed with knives and boxcutters. Carried out with ridiculously simple means, the New York and Washington attacks shocked America and caused, directly or indirectly, damages estimated at more than 60 billion dollars.[163]

But the most important asymmetry is psychological: an immense gap separates men for whom there are many things worse than death and a world in which individual life, a purely subjective fact, is regarded as the most valuable of all goods. Today's Westerners live in a 'disenchanted' world which considers nothing more valuable than life. Historically, this sentiment has been the exception rather than the rule. Percy Kemp speaks here very correctly of the 'anthropocentric choice which was made, starting from the Renaissance, of placing

---

161 *Les logiques du terrorisme*, p. 29.

162 'The participants in asymmetric conflicts are all definitely "transnationals,"' declares Zygmunt Bauman. 'They are also in their behaviour: mobile, assigned to no place, they easily change their target and recognise no border' (*La société assiégée* [Rodez: Le Rouergue/Chambon, 2005], p. 142, English translation: *Society Under Siege* [Cambridge: Polity, 2002]). He adds, 'The truly asymmetric wars are an event concurrent with globalisation. Custom-built for the global space and brought onto the global scene, they explicitly despise territorial ambitions' (ibid., p.146). Cf. also Zygmunt Bauman, 'Wars of the Globalization Era,' in *European Journal of Social Theory* IV, 2001, 1, pp. 11-28.

163 On the concept of asymmetric war, cf. Jorge Verstrynge, *La guerra periférica y el islam revolucionario: Orígenes, reglas y ética de la guerra asimétrica* (Madrid: El Viejo Topo, 2005).

man rather than God at the centre of the universe and of substituting the fear of death for the fear of hell.'[164] Hence the radical asymmetry between terrorists ready to give their lives while taking the lives of others, precisely because they do not have a 'fear of death,' and those for whom this behaviour is strictly 'incomprehensible' since for them life is more valuable than anything else. It is this asymmetry which tends to make victims describe terrorism as smacking of an 'absurd nihilism': the rationality of the secularised Western world makes it incapable of understanding motivations deriving from a logic which this world itself knew in the past, that is, that there are causes, good or bad of course, which are worth giving one's life for. The refusal to consider life absolutely sacred, the absence of a 'fear of death,' can arise, from this point of view, only from a 'fanaticism' identifiable with criminal madness. Between those who think of the world to come and those who think of their retirement there can be no common ground. For the terrorists, death is, in the final analysis, a reward. In the face of this desire for death established as an absolute weapon, the West is inevitably defenceless.

Terrorism is, finally, asymmetrical also in the sense that it manages to have a formidable impact on opinion even when killing relatively few people — infinitely fewer, for example, than the numerous 'ordinary' murders occurring every year throughout the world.[165] It is, from this point of view, somewhat comparable to aviation disasters, which are rare but always widely publicised because they cause the simultaneous deaths of several dozens or hundreds of people. In comparison, car accidents, which collectively kill infinitely more people, but only a few at once, seldom receive much attention. Terrorism also causes fewer deaths than ethnic massacres such as occurred in Rwanda, for example, but it evokes stronger reactions because it is more spectacular. This character as spectacle is indissociable from the objective that it assigns to itself. Its true impact is psychological.

---

164 Percy Kemp, 'Terroristes, ou anges vengeurs,' p. 19. Zygmunt Bauman notes also that the path traversed by Western civilisation confirms, among other things, 'the rapidity with which the will to sacrifice one's life for a cause has been condemned and classified as a symptom of religious fanaticism, cultural retardation or barbarism, by countries which, for several centuries, presented martyrdom as being evidence of sainthood and giving the right to beatification' (*La société assiégée*, p. 148).

165 In the space of three decades, terrorism has caused the death of a little fewer than 20,000 persons.

Global terrorism aims in fact at the weakening of structures and the destabilisation of behaviour. Referring to recent terrorist actions, Pierre Mannoni writes very correctly that the purpose of the men behind them is not so much to 'drag the masses out of their apathy,' 'as in the period of historical revolutions, as of plunging them into it and of inhibiting their faculties of defence or initiative.'[166] For his part, Jordan Paust observed, already in the 1960s, that the desired objective of terrorist attacks was 'to use intense fear or anxiety to coerce the primary target into behaviour or to mould its attitudes in connection with a demanded power (political) outcome.'[167] This definition shows well that the 'principal target' is never that which is aimed at straight-away, but that which one wishes to hit as it were on the rebound (it is in this that the terrorist act is similar to kidnapping). Already during the terror bombings of the civilian German or Japanese populations during the Second World War, the target aimed at beyond the victims themselves were the German or Japanese governments. It is the same with global terrorism, whose actions aim more for a *secondary* effect than a primary one: the attacks are only means of shaping public opinion or putting pressure on the politics of governments. Terrorism thus wishes to influence minds and disarm wills. The desired objec-tive of 11 September, for example, was not so much to destroy the Twin Towers of New York as to traumatise public opinion by the spectacle of their destruction. This is an important difference in relation to the partisan or the guerrilla fighter who seeks almost always to achieve direct effects on immediate objectives, the primary effect being the effect sought.

In today's world, this objective is obtained mainly through the mass media. There is, in fact, a clear link between the intrinsically spectacu-lar character of the great terrorist attacks and the sensation they cause in the media. Terrorism strikes the eyes as much as it impresses the imagination. It is by presenting a disturbing spectacle arousing strong emotions and immediate visceral reactions that terrorism is able to shock: the attacks of 11 September were the perfect illustration of that. The development of terrorism is intimately related to the expansion of the international media system which, by reporting such events

---

166 Les logiques du terrorisme, p. 10.
167 'A Definitional Focus,' in Yonah Alexander and Seymour Maxwell Finger (eds.), *Terrorism: Interdisciplinary Perspectives* (New York: John Jay Press, 1977), p. 21.

in 'real time,' multiplies their impact. The shock effect of an attack does not depend so much on its actual scope as on what will be said about it: if no one speaks of it, it is as if it had not taken place. As Paul Virilio remarks quite correctly, 'The weapon of mass communication is strategically superior to the weapon of mass destruction.'[168] There is a sort of perverse but organic link between terrorism and the media, a link which resembles the way advertising language tends to establish itself as a paradigm of all social language.[169] 'Terrorism operates at a symbolic as well as a material level,' writes Rüdiger Safranski, 'there are terrorist actions but also, equally important, terrible news. This is why the media become unwilling accomplices. Some sow terror in the expectation that others will spread it. [...] [T]he use of media messages is part and parcel of modern terrorism.'[170] Terrorism thus constitutes a murderous game of four: the terrorists, the victims, the 'principal target' (the established powers) and the media.

Shortly before his death, Jacques Derrida posed this question: 'How does a terror that is organized, provoked, and instrumentalized differ from this *fear* that an entire tradition, from Hobbes to Schmitt and even to Benjamin, holds to be the very condition of the authority of law and of the sovereign exercise of power, the very condition of the political and of the state?'[171] In a general sense, the statement was without doubt contestable, but it at least had the merit of putting the emphasis on the concept of fear. In global terrorism the fear of danger is, in fact, even more important than the danger. The terrorist is an enemy reputed to be capable of everything, but 'invisible' and therefore virtually omnipresent.[172] This characteristic serves him to the extent that it contributes to amplify the effect of the desired fear. Not recognising any limits or measures, or being restricted to any

---

168 'L'état d'urgence permanent,' p. 96.

169 Cf. Yonah Alexander and Richard Latter (eds.), *Terrorism and the Media: Dilemmas for Government, Journalists and the Public* (Washington: Brassey's,1990; and Pierre Mannoni, *Un laboratoire de la peur: terrorisme et médias* (Marseille: Hommes et perspectives, 1992).

170 Rüdiger Safranski, *How Much Globalization Can We Bear?* (Cambridge: Polity Press, 2005), p. 46-47.

171 'Autoimmunity: Real and Symbolic Suicides: A Dialogue with Jacques Derrida,' p. 102.

172 George W. Bush, writes François-Bernard Huyghe, 'is the first to conduct his principal combat against a danger which does not reside in the power of the adversary, but in the moral perversity of an invisible group' ('Le terrorisme, le mal et la démocratie,' in *Le Monde*, 18 February 2005).

particular means, terrorism destroys all criteria, for it derives from a logic radically different from the current rationality. Its 'invisibility,' its unpredictability, increase the fear aroused by the threat that it constitutes, at the same time that it gives rise to all sorts of conspiracy theories. In a society where (omnipresent) *risk* has taken the place of (identifiable and locally present) *danger*,[173] it engenders a climate of general suspicion which tends to legitimate any control measures or restrictions, and make people willing to sacrifice freedoms to see that they are guaranteed more security.

We said above that terrorism is war in peacetime, or even a war *as peace* — and it is a 'global' and total war. At the end of September 2001, the White House code-named its plan for a war on terrorism 'infinite justice.'[174] Now, by definition, 'infinite justice' does not know any limits. George W. Bush, addressing Congress, declared at the same time that this war would not end 'until every terrorist group of global reach has been found, stopped and defeated.'[175] 'We desire a total victory in Iraq, and we will have a total victory,' he further explained, which clearly signified that everything short of total victory would be considered total defeat. In other words, this undeclared war is a war without end. Paul Virilio wrote that 'with terrorism, we have entered the era of war without end, in both senses of the word.'[176] It is at once a war which cannot be terminated and a war without a precise aim or determined objective.[177] It is endless from both sides'

---

173 Cf. Ulrich Beck, *Risikogesellschaft: Auf dem Weg in eine andere Moderne* (Frankfurt: Suhrkamp, 1986) (French translation: *La société du risque* (Paris: Aubier, 2001); English translation: *Risk Society: Towards a New Modernity* (London: Sage, 1992). Cf. also Jane Franklin (ed.), *The Politics of the Risk Society* (Oxford: Polity Press, 1998); and Corey Robin, *La peur: Histoire d'une idée politique* (Paris: Armand Colin, 2006).

174 Operation Infinite Justice was the name initially given to military operations in Afghanistan. However, upon learning that this name would be offensive to Muslims, who believe that only God can dispense ultimate justice, the name was changed to Operation Enduring Freedom on 25 September 2001, before the operations commenced.-Ed.

175 Address to the U.S. Congress, 20 September 2001.-Ed.

176 'L'état d'urgence permanent,' p. 97. Cf. also Enrique Dussel, 'Estado de guerra permanente y razón cinica,' in *Herramienta: Revista de debate y crítica marxista* 21, Winter-Spring 2002-03.

177 'Global terrorism is extreme,' observes Jürgen Habermas for his part, 'both in its lack of realistic goals and in its cynical exploitation of the vulnerability of complex systems.' ('Fundamentalism and Terror: A Dialogue with Jürgen Habermas,' interview with Giovanna Borradori, in *Philosophy in a Time of Terror*, p. 34).

point of view, because the terrorists cannot seriously hope to defeat their adversaries, while the latter cannot seriously hope to make terrorism disappear completely. By definition, the war against terrorism cannot be lost or won. As Carl Schmitt predicted, global terrorism has a bright future ahead of it.

3. From a 'Case of Emergency' to a Permanent State of Emergency

Confronted with terrorism, the old doctrine of 'containment' has become obsolete. The battle against terrorism has become an offensive and preventive battle. It implies a right of unlimited pursuit which, in authorising the pursuer to cross borders, enables him at the same time to affirm his hegemony over the world.[178] But it is also a matter of emergency, and therefore ends in a state of emergency. Characteristic of 'times of distress,' the state of emergency is related to that 'state of necessity' which the historian Theodor Mommsen compared with legitimate defence. In the state of emergency, a state finds itself suddenly confronted with an extreme danger, a mortal threat which it can face only by resorting to means which cannot be justified in normal times according to its own standards. The emergency situation or state of emergency is defined as the dramatic occurrence of unusual events or of unpredictable situations which, on account of their threatening character, demand to be dealt with immediately by resorting to measures that are themselves exceptional (restriction of freedoms, martial law, state of siege, etc.), but are considered to be the only ones suited for the situation.

The concept of the 'emergency case' (*Ernstfall*) or state of emergency (*Ausnahmezustand*)[179] plays a central role in the political and constitutional theory of Carl Schmitt, where it is related to his critique of liberalism.[180] For Schmitt, the emergency being unpredictable, it is

---

178 'By taking over from other forms of less consensual or efficient interference (humanitarian, human rights, war against drugs or organised crime), [the anti-terrorist] war allows one to envisage anew expansion on a planetary level,' writes Percy Kemp. 'In this sense, it is a warlike counterpart to the world economic market' ('Terroristes, ou anges vengeurs,' pp. 22-23).

179 The word means, literally, 'exceptional situation.'-Ed.

180 This concept is principally studied in the first of the four chapters of the *Political Theology* of 1922: *Politische Theologie: Vier Kapitel zur Lehre von der Souveränität* (Munich-Leipzig: Duncker & Humblot, 1922). Latest edition: Berlin 2004, French translation: 'Théologie politique: Quatre chapitres sur la théorie de la souveraineté,' in *Théologie politique 1922, 1969* (Paris: Gallimard, 1988), pp. 9-75; English

futile to believe that it is possible to determine beforehand the means to respond to it. Liberalism, if it is inspired by Neo-Kantian formalism[181] or Kelsenian positivism,[182] cannot understand the nature of the emergency nor confront it without betraying itself, because it adheres to a strictly procedural or juridico-formal conception of the social order, which claims that a pre-established rule or norm can be applied to any situation whatsoever, which historical experience belies.

By suspending the legal norm, adds Carl Schmitt, the emergency helps one to better understand the nature of politics, in the sense that it shows where sovereignty — that is, the concrete capacity of making decisions when faced with an unexpected situation — resides. The state of emergency reveals simultaneously the authority and the place of sovereignty at the same time that it causes the decision (*Entscheidung*) to appear in its 'absolute purity.' The sovereign political authority is not necessarily synonymous with the state. '*Souverän ist, wer über den Ausnahmezustand entscheidet,*'[183] writes Carl Schmitt. This formula, which has become famous, can be understood in two ways: the one who decides in an exceptional situation is sovereign, but also the one who decides on the exception itself is sovereign, that is, the one who decides that the situation is no longer normal and that the ordinary rules no longer apply. There is therefore a close link between the exception and the decision that Schmitt identifies as the

---

translation: *Political Theology: Four Chapters on the Concept of Sovereignty* (Cambridge:, MIT Press, Cambridge 1985). For a critique of recent events, cf. Tom Sorell, 'Schmitt's and Hobbesian Politics of Emergency,' in Luc Foisneau, Jean-Christophe Merle and Tom Sorell (eds.), *Leviathan Between the Wars: Hobbes' Impact on Early Twentieth Century Political Philosophy* (Frankfurt: Peter Lang, 2005), pp. 95-107. For a general approach to the question within the framework of German constitutional law, cf. András Jakab, 'German Constitutional Law and Doctrine on State of Emergency – Paradigms and Dilemmas of a Traditional (Contintela) Discourse,' in *German Law Journal*, May 2006, pp. 453-477.

181 Neo-Kantian formalism is based on the assumption that the purpose of ethics is to determine one's imperative, or more specifically, what one is obliged to do according to one's duty. One determines one's duty by proceeding from the idea that the way in which one makes moral decisions proceeds from the concept that one should act according to values that are universally valid, and which should therefore be adopted by all rational beings.-Ed.

182 Hans Kelsen (1881-1973) was a jurist who developed his own school of legal positivist thought. He postulated that within every legal system is a *Grundnorm*, or 'basic norm,' which he believed to be an unchanging norm underlying all the outward realities and manifestations of its day-to-day workings.-Ed.

183 'Sovereign is he who decides on the exception.' The first sentence of *Political Theology*, p. 5.-Ed.

'first cause' of every political society or body. Schmitt sees in the decision in the exceptional (or emergency) case the purest expression of
the political act: the suspension of the legal norms in an exceptional
case constitutes the ultimate manifestation of political sovereignty.
Sovereignty, he emphasises, is in fact not so much the power of laying
down the law as the power of suspending it. But one would be wrong
to interpret this statement as an apology for arbitrariness. On the one
hand, Schmitt emphasises that in deciding in a case of emergency,
the sovereign is not free to act according to his own good pleasure,
but that he is, on the contrary, obliged to act in a way that takes into
consideration his responsibilities. On the other hand, he affirms that
the exception defines the rule in the sense that one cannot understand
a rule without taking its limits into consideration, that is, the circumstances that can make it inapplicable. In other words: the one who
decides the exception to the norm also defines the norm. 'The exception is more interesting than the rule,' writes Schmitt in his *Political
Theology*. 'The rule proves nothing; the exception proves everything:
It confirms not only the rule but also its existence, which derives only
from the exception.'[184]

The state of emergency is also important because it reveals the
originally non-normative character of the law. It is not justice (*Recht*)
as such that is suspended in the state of emergency, but only the normative element of the law (*Gesetz*). The state of emergency reveals
thereby the existential character of the law. The exception is essential,
not because it is rare, but because it is unpredictable. Just as the enemy
himself, who cannot be determined *a priori* by a pre-existing general
norm — for hostility is always related to the concrete context of the
moment — it cannot therefore be codified in advance. In relating the
law to its non-juridical source, in the case of the sovereign decision,
Schmitt attacks all forms of constitutional rationalism, notably the
theory of the rule of law or positivist theory, according to which the
sovereign should always respect the law, no matter what the circumstances. The occurrence of an emergency situation, and its implica-
tions, demonstrate that that is quite simply not possible, since the
norm cannot foresee the exception. A constitution remains, in this
sense, always incomplete. At most it can foresee a situation in which
it would not be applied.

184 *Political Theology*, p. 15.

But Schmitt emphasises also that the exception is by definition exceptional, that is, it cannot be transformed into a state of permanent reality. The exception is to the rule or to the norm what war is to peace. Just like the ancient Roman dictatorship, the suspension of the norm by the sovereign can therefore only be temporary. It can also open a new cycle of law. In his book on *Dictatorship*,[185] Schmitt clearly states that dictatorship, which can be justified in certain cases, suspends the norms currently in force but does not change the legal order or the nature of the state, which means that it has legitimacy only insofar as it aims at restoring the rule of law. Dictatorship then remains a constitutional dictatorship: the suspension of the legal order does not mean its abolition.[186] In an emergency situation, if the state suspends the legal rules, it is with a view to conserving them. The decision on the exception thereby proves itself to be a decision on the concrete conditions of the norm's application. '[A] normal situation must exist,' writes Schmitt, 'and he is sovereign who decides definitively if this normal situation exists really.'[187]

The theory of the emergency case shows the always eminently *concrete* character of Schmittian thought: if he rejects abstract formal theories, it is because he is mindful of the context (and here it should be recalled that it was in consideration of the troubled circumstances in his own country between 1917 and 1919 that Schmitt enunciated his doctrine). In the Weimar Republic's Constitution of 1919, the famous Article 48, to which Schmitt devoted many writings, defines the state of emergency in constitutional terms. This article, quite comparable to Article 16 of the constitution of the French Fifth Republic, endows the president with extraordinary powers to confront exceptional situations, including the right to call on the armed forces to put and end

---

185 *Die Diktatur: Von den Anfängen des modernen Souveränitätsgedankens bis zum proletarischen Klassenkampf* (Munich-Leipzig: Duncker & Humblot, 1921); latest edition: Berlin 1994; French translation: *La dictature*, Seuil, Paris 2000; English translation: *Dictatorship* (Cambridge: Polity, 2010).

186 It is the same idea that one finds in Machiavelli (when he cites the example of Cincinnatus) and, in modern times, in the famous work of Clinton L. Rossiter, *Constitutional Dictatorship: Crisis Government in the Modern Democracies* (Princeton: Princeton University Press, 1948).

187 *Political Theology*, p. 13.

to serious unrest or internal disorder. This Article 48 was invoked more than 250 times under the Weimar Republic![188]

But the notion of the state of emergency is not peculiar to Germany or France. A study published in 1978 estimated that, at that time, at least 30 countries were in a state of emergency.[189] The American constitution itself foresees the suspension of the writ of *habeas corpus* 'when in Cases of Rebellion or Invasion the public Safety may require it' (Article 1, Section 9, Clause 2), but instead of making it a privilege of the executive power, it grants this suspensive power to Congress. During the Civil War, Abraham Lincoln decided to suspend *habeas corpus* without referring the question to Congress, just as after the attack on Pearl Harbor, Franklin D. Roosevelt had Americans of Japanese origin interned in camps as a preventive measure. During the Cold War, the confrontation with the Soviet Union also led the United States to adopt certain exceptional measures considered to be justified by the demands of 'national security.' One can cite here the National Security Act of 1947 which, starting at that time, placed the concept of 'national security' at the centre of American preoccupations in matters of foreign policy. Several studies have been devoted to the constitutional effects of the Cold War.[190] Exceptional measures were taken also in the domain of domestic policy in the McCarthy era, which resulted in the systematic reinterpretation of the rights of American citizens and the adoption of surveillance of citizens sus-

---

188 One will nevertheless note that the conditions of application of this article have always remained vague, inasmuch as Article 48 stipulated that the declaration of the state of emergency by the president had to be ratified by the parliament, whereas Article 25 gave the president the right to dissolve the parliament.

189 John Ferejohn and Pasquale Pasquino, 'The Law of the Exception: A Typology of Emergency Powers,' in *International Journal of Constitutional Law*, 2004, 2, pp. 210-239, go so far as to make the constitutional possibility of suspending the law a characteristic feature of the 'non-absolutist Western legal tradition.' In 1948, Clinton L. Rossiter writes in his book *Constitutional Dictatorship*: 'No sacrifice is too great for our democracy, least of all the temporary sacrifice of democracy itself' (p. 314). He enumerates later eleven conditions for a temporary dictatorship to remain constitutional. These views have been recently discussed by David Dyzenhaus in a text entitled 'Schmitt v Dicey: Are States of Emergency Inside or Outside the Legal Order?.' Cf. also G.L. Negretto and J. A. A. Rivera, 'Liberalism and Emergency Powers in Latin America: Reflections on Carl Schmitt and the Theory of Constitutional Dictatorship,' in *Cardozo Law Review*, 2000, 5-6, pp. 1797-1824; and Bruce Ackerman, 'The Emergency Constitution,' in *Yale Law Journal* CXIII, 2004, pp. 1029-1076.

190 Cf., notably, Daniel Yergin, *Shattered Peace: The Origins of the Cold War and the National Security State* (Boston: Houghton Mifflin, 1977).

pected of harbouring Communist sympathies. The Internal Security Act of 1950 even provided for the creation of six provisional internment camps (which were never used for this purpose) that could be used in an emergency case. Between 1950 and 1970 Congress adopted no less than 470 clauses aimed at reinforcing the executive power to confront exceptional situations. None of these clauses was abrogated after the dismantling of the Soviet Union.

The measures taken by the American government immediately after the attacks of 11 September thus have precedents. But they also have particular characteristics which differentiate them radically from the Schmittian 'model.' To the extent to which they allegedly confront a danger — global terrorism — on which the authorities of the United States have declared a war which, as we have seen above, strongly risks being endless, they clearly tend to become definitively institutionalised, in other words, to last indefinitely. The state of emergency then stops being exceptional and becomes permanent.

For certain authors, the development of terrorism before 11 September could already have justified the declaration of a state of emergency.[191] After this date, in any case, things have accelerated. Immediately after the attacks, George W. Bush declared a state of emergency, following which the Congress adopted a resolution authorising the President 'to use all necessary and appropriate force against those nations, organizations, or persons he determines planned, authorized, committed, or aided the terrorist attacks that occurred on September 11, 2001, or harboured such organizations or persons, in order to prevent any future acts of international terrorism against the United States by such nations, organizations or persons.'[192] A month later, on 24 October 2001, the USA PATRIOT Act (acronym for 'Uniting and Strengthening America by Providing Appropriate Tools Required to Intercept and Obstruct Terrorism') was approved with a resounding majority by the House of Representatives. It authorised the FBI to conduct secret investigations into the private lives of persons suspected of terrorism, to hack into their computers without their

---

191 Cf. William B. Scheuerman, 'Globalization and Exceptional Powers: The Erosion of Liberal Democracy,' in *Radical Philosophy*, 1999; and Oren Gross, 'On Terrorism and Other Criminals: States of Emergency and the Criminal Legal System,' in Eliezer Lederman (ed.), *New Trends in Criminal Law*, 2000.

192 *Authorization for Use of Military Force*, Section 2, Clause A, proclamation no. 7463, 14 September 2001.

knowledge, and to use surveillance software to indefinitely store the records of their Internet browsing. It also authorised the Department of Justice to have any foreigner suspected of being a threat to national security arrested and placed in detention.[193] Finally, on 13 November 2001, President Bush also signed a Military Order envisaging bringing presumed terrorists before a special military court and detaining suspects indefinitely.

These emergency laws have provided for searching the homes of suspects without a warrant, as well as for having suspects arrested and indefinitely detained, deported, or imprisoned in solitary confinement without charge or trial. They have led to the creation of zones where ordinary laws do not apply and to certain individuals being deprived of legal status. The FBI and the National Security Agency (NSA) have in fact been granted virtually unlimited powers, exempt from all judicial control, in matters of surveillance of communications both in the United States and abroad. More than 1,200 foreigners were arrested on mere suspicions. Four months later, 900 of them were still incarcerated, without any specific charges having being brought against them, without having had an opportunity to argue their case before a judge or to obtain legal counsel.[194] The 'Military Order' of 13 November 2001 envisaged that suspects would not be informed of who had accused them, that the accused would not be allowed the right of appeal and that the right to a legal defence would be 'severely limited.' The trials would take place behind closed doors in military bases or on warships. Sentences would be pronounced

---

193 In November 2003, Congress voted an amendment to the USA PATRIOT Act ('Patriot II') which allows federal agencies to demand that Internet providers disclose personal information on any Internet user without being subject to judicial control. Besides, the 'Domestic Security Enhancement Act' of 2003 permits the withdrawal of American nationality from any citizen accused of terrorism, thus granting to the authorities a discretionary power regarding the recognition of citizenship. The arrangements foreseen by the USA PATRIOT Act were renewed in 2005. For the details of these measures, cf. Kim Lane Scheppele, 'Law in a Time of Emergency: States of Exception and the Temptations of 9/11,' in *Journal of Constitutional Law*, May 2004, pp. 1-75 (text republished on 1 October 2004 in the form of a brochure, University of Pennsylvania Law School, Scholarship at Penn Law, Paper 55). The author specifies that he is examining the circumstances in which these measures were taken 'in the light of the writings of Carl Schmitt on the nature of the state of emergency.'

194 In England, the Anti-Terrorism, Crime and Security Act of 2001 also permitted the indefinite incarceration of foreigners suspected of terrorism. A ruling of the Law Lords subsequently declared their detention without charge or trial illegal.

by a commission composed entirely of officers, unanimity no longer being required to condemn the accused to death, and with no possibility of appeal. The judicial procedure would take place in secret, and conversations between the accused and his counsel could be secretly recorded.

One of the most spectacular consequences of this range of measures has been the internment in a camp situated on the American military base of Guantánamo, in Cuba, of several hundred detainees (of more than 40 different nationalities) who may be kept there indefinitely without having been charged or even knowing what they are accused of, without access to counsel and without benefiting from the clauses of the Geneva Convention relating to the treatment of prisoners of war.[195] These detainees, having been taken prisoner in Afghanistan, Iraq or elsewhere, have been accorded a status of 'illegal enemy combatants' which is devoid of all juridical value or content. Interned without judgement, the prisoners of Guantánamo are in fact neither detained under common law, nor are they political prisoners, nor are they prisoners of war. A number of them have been badly treated and subjected to brutalities. Some of them have subsequently been transferred to allied countries with little consideration for human rights in order to be systematically tortured there.[196] The Guantánamo camp is, in fact, from a legal point of view, a 'grey zone' quite comparable to the 'grey zone' where traffickers of narcotics act. The 2005 annual report of Amnesty International, made public on 25 May 2005, did not hesitate to describe it as 'the Gulag of our times.'[197]

---

195 The conventions of the Hague and Geneva notably stipulate that civilian populations should never be seen as targets, that prisoners should be well treated, that certain arms are prohibited, and so forth. Concerning the persons suspected of terrorism, these arrangements have been officially declared to be 'obsolete' by Alberto Gonzales, adviser to the White House, who subsequently went on to become Attorney General. Regarding the Iraq War, Michael Walzer notes that 'Rumsfeld's Pentagon delivered the Iraqi prisoners to reservists who had never heard of the Geneva Convention' (De la guerre et du terrorisme, p. 216).

196 Cf. Stephen Grey, 'Délocalisation de la torture,' in Le Monde diplomatique, April 2005, pp. 1 & 10-11.

197 On the Guantánamo prison, cf. Emmanuelle Bribosia and Anne Weyembergh, Lutte contre le terrorisme et droits fondamentaux (Brussels: Bruylant, 2003; David Abraham, 'The Bush Regime from Elections to Detentions: A Moral Economy of Carl Schmitt and Human Rights,' University of Miami, October 2006; David P. Forsythe, 'United States Policy toward Enemy Detaines in the "War on Terrrorism",' in Human Rights Quarterly, 2006, pp. 465-491; and Moazzam Begg and Victoria Brittain, Enemy Combatant (London: Pocket Books, 2006). Cf. also Erik Saar and Viveca

In the name of the war on terrorism and the holy alliance against a common imminent threat, numerous public freedoms have thus been suspended in America. 'Civil liberties have been limited,' writes Jean-Claude Marquerie, president of the High Court of Paris, 'and guarantees against the attacks on fundamental rights considerably reduced. Thousands of suspects, American and (especially) foreigners have found themselves deprived of all defence, all rights, and all judgement.'[198] Consequently, a climate of fear has been continuously cultivated, favouring on many occasions new attacks on personal freedoms. From public authorities, the most frequent allegation has been that of 'threats' affecting 'national security,' two concepts that certainly evoke a feeling of urgency or emergency, but which both remain equally vague, facilitating their political and legal exploitation as well as their use as a pretext to curtail freedoms. One notes, besides, the constant broadening of the concept of 'national security,' which first possessed essentially military connotations, but which has come to encompass, step by step, every aspect of social or international life.

The anti-terrorist fight invariably raises the question of whether democracies can, in exceptional cases, employ methods against terrorists that are condemned in normal times. The most common such method is torture.[199] The tortures of the Abu Ghraib prison are in

Novak, *Inside the Wire: A Military Intelligence Soldier's Eyewitness Account of Life at Guantánamo* (London: Penguin Press, 2005). Erik Saar is a young sergeant of the American army who was himself stationed at Guantánamo for six months. For his part, Fleur Johns, 'Guantánamo Bay and the Annihilation of the Exception,' in *European Journal of International Law* XVI, 4, September 2005, pp. 613-635, paradoxically maintains that this prison is part of the norm and not of the exception, by proposing a very heterodox reading of the theses of Carl Schmitt. In November 2003, the Supreme Court of the United States accepted to decide on the legality of the detention of the foreigners interned at Guantánamo. On 28 June 2004 it declared that the Guantánamo base was indeed placed under the jurisdiction of the United States and granted the detainees the right to contest their imprisonment before an American tribunal. But, by giving them this right, it thereby also recognised the exceptional right created by the American executive power. The Supreme Court did not in fact pronounce on the conditions of detention of the internees. As Jean-Claude Paye remarked, 'It simply gives the prisoners the right to appeal to a federal judge, without guaranteeing them formal access to an attorney. It thus legitimates procedures derogatory to the stages of detention and judgement. At this latter level, it installs a veritable system of reversal of the burden of proof, since it is the prisoners who must convince the judges that they are not guilty of these charges' ('Le droit pénal comme un acte constituant: Une mutation du droit pénal,' p. 282).

198 'Terrorisme et droits de l'homme,' in *Le Monde*, 1 March 2005.

199 One has enough information and evidence today to know that, within the framework of the Iraq War and the war against terrorism, the recourse to torture has been

fact not just a result of the 'culture of shamelessness' denounced by Susan Sontag. The debates that followed the publication of the books of Paul Berman, *Terror and Liberalism*, and Michael Ignatieff, *The Lesser Evil*[200] bear witness to that. Ignatieff, director of the Carr Center for Human Rights at Harvard University, brings to light the manner in which terrorism leads many people to consider as so many weaknesses the characteristic traits of liberal democracies of which they used to pride themselves (tolerance, pluralism, respect for freedoms, etc.). Observing that 'human rights are not a system of indivisible absolutes,' he emphasises that democracies must certainly protect individual rights, but also guarantee their collective existence, tasks that are not easily reconciled.[201]

Kim Lane Scheppele shows for his part that the emergency measures adopted by the Bush administration were taken, not only in consideration of a state of emergency at the national level, but also at the international level, and above all that these measures have not stopped proliferating. The important point is evidently there. Whereas in the emergency case of the 'classical' type, such as Carl Schmitt defines it, the measures adopted to confront an emergency situation are generally of short duration and permit a progressive return to the normal, in the case of the measures taken in the aftermath of September 11, we see an entire system of emergency which has subsequently been gradually reinforced. 'The greater abuses,' writes Scheppele, 'have come as 9/11 recedes and executive policy has turned toward larger and larger constitutional exceptions, with the active acquiescence so far of both Congress and the courts.'[202]

---

constant. Cf. Sanford Levinson, 'Torture in Iraq and the Rule of Law in America,' in *Daedalus*, 2004, 3, pp. 5-9.

200 Paul Berman, *Terror and Liberalism* (New York: W. W. Norton, 2003); and Michael Ignatieff, *The Lesser Evil: Politics and Ethics in an Age of Terror* (Princeton: Princeton University Press, 2004).

201 Cf. also Susie Linfield, 'La danse des civilisations: l'Orient, l'Occident et Abu Ghraib,' in *Esprit*, June 2005, pp. 66-84, who wonders if a country can 'fight efficiently against terrorist groups without having recourse at times to extrajudicial techniques abroad, or without being led to limit the freedoms on its own territory' (p. 78).

202 Kim Lane Scheppele, 'Law in a Time of Emergency: States of Exception and the Temptations of 9/11,' p. 3. The author analyses, besides, the reasons why the European countries, though themselves confronted by the threat of terrorism, have not engaged in the same direction. Her conclusion, which can be disputed, is that 'the Schmittian conception of emergency is, for a great number of our allies, in particular European, no longer considered as an acceptable framework of response'

This conclusion is shared by many observers[203] who take the view that the definition of terrorism used by the government is very extensive, since it takes into account both acts and intentions. This vagueness permits the criminalisation of certain behaviours, the generalisation of suspicion, the justification of measures of preventive detention, the limitation of communication between the accused and their counsel, and so on. Though anti-terrorist legislation is primarily directed against persons suspected of terrorism, it indirectly affects the entire population, bringing about a veritable upheaval in the criminal law. But the battle between 'Good' and 'Evil,' a very frequent subject of public discourse in the United States, also serves as a diversion. It masks the social insecurity and projects externally the internal contradictions of the country that makes use of it. The discussion of 'internal security' prolongs the discussion of the 'national security' by relating it to civil society. The use of the term 'security' in an increasingly wider sense is accompanied by a tendency to remove from the public debate all the problems relating to it, ending thus in a new form of 'depoliticisation.' The curtailment of freedoms is made possible by the citizens' expectations: their desire for security takes precedence over their desire for freedom. This is all the more the case in a world where threats are at the same time omnipresent and difficult to identify. Concomitantly, the war against terrorism allows, at the international level, the reinforcement of the authority of the

(ibid.). On this point, cf. Alexandre Adam, *La lutte contre le terrorisme. Etude comparative Union européenne/Etats-Unis*, L'Harmattan, Paris 2005.

203 Cf. Adrien Masset, 'Terrorisme et libertés publiques,' in Quentin Michel (ed.), *Terrorisme — Terrorism: Regards croisés — Cross Analysis* (Pieterlen: Peter Lang, 2005). On the consequences of the adoption of the 'Patriot Act' for the citizens of the United States, cf. George Steinmetz, 'The State of Emergency and the Revival of Modern American Imperialism: Toward an Authoritarian Post-Fordism,' in *Public Culture*, Spring 2003, pp. 323-345; M. C. Williams, 'Words, Images, Enemies: Securitization and International Politics,' in *International Studies Quarterly* XLVII, 4, December 2003, pp. 511-531; Andrew Norris, '"Us" and "Them",'; Bernd Hamm (ed.), *Devastating Society: The Neo-Conservative Assault on Democracy and Justice,* (London: Pluto Press, 2005); Robert Harvey & Hélène Volat, *USA Patriot Act: De l'exception à la règle* (Paris: Lignes-Manifestes, 2006); and David Keen, *Endless War? Hidden Functions of the War on Terror* (London: Pluto Press, 2006). For a reading (inspired by Deleuze) of the 'war against terrorism' as a 'hypermodern intensification of the technological and militarised rationales of modernity,' cf. John Armitage, 'On Ernst Jünger's "Total Mobilization": A Re-evaluation in the Era of the War on Terrorism,' in *Body & Society*, 2003, 4, pp. 191-213.

dominant American power, presented as being best suited to provide 'global protection.'[204]

Finally, terrorism provides the state, which previously appeared increasingly impotent in the face of global influences and challenges linked to globalisation, with a new legitimacy and a new role. We shall not elaborate on this subject, but one may ask if the state—which Carl Schmitt clearly saw already in the 1930s would not remain the privileged locus of politics—is not in the process of rediscovering a new legitimacy by means of its supposed capacity to provide security and to fight terrorism. The emergency measures adopted recently in the United States and elsewhere should be seen in this context. These measures have, on the one hand, evident extensions at the international level, the fight against terrorism demanding transnational cooperation of police forces and intelligence services (and from this point of view, the anti-terrorist fight is perfectly in keeping with globalisation). But they undoubtedly give back a role to a state structure set to become increasingly obsolete, the national elites finding 'in the war against terror a choice point of operations for perpetuating their power and introducing a large range of laws allowing them to impose themselves on both their enemies and their own civil society.'[205] The state, in other words, is no longer legitimised except by its capacity to provide security and, at the same time, it uses the irrepressible desire for security to reinforce its control by restraining freedoms. As Jean Baudrillard has rightly remarked, '[I]t is the real victory of terrorism that it has plunged the whole of the West into the obsession with security—that is to say, into a veiled form of perpetual terror.'[206]

One cannot be surprised that the name of Carl Schmitt has been frequently cited in these commentaries and critiques. 'The attack on 11 September 2001,' remarks Jean-Claude Monod, 'perhaps confirms the link sensed by Schmitt between the—literally—theological understanding of the enemy and the figure of the "motorised partisan," who manages in this case to turn against the emblematic power

---

204 The will to enlist, under the flag of the international antiterrorist battle, allies who are increasingly more reluctant since the end of the Cold War to accept the American leadership, goes back to at least Bill Clinton, if not to Ronald Reagan.

205 Percy Kemp, 'Terroristes, ou anges vengeurs,' p. 22.

206 Cf. Jean Baudrillard, *L'esprit du terrorisme* (Paris: Galilée, 2001); English translation: *The Spirit of Terrorism and Other Essays* (London: Verso, 2003), p. 81.

the very element of its power — the air.'[207] Although hostile to the
ideas of Schmitt, the author nevertheless emphasises that the critique
of the German jurist assumes 'a particularly glaring topicality when
the White House decrees the doctrine of "preventive war" [and] trans-
gresses the rules of international law to conduct a "war for peace"
which is described in theological terms like "crusade" and confrontation with the "axis of evil."'[208]

'Anti-terrorist legislation,' writes Jean-Claude Paye, 'ensures the
domination of the emergency procedures. Thus, the traditional role
of criminal procedure is reversed. Instead of being a framework for
protecting public and private freedoms, it becomes the means by
which the latter are systematically violated. In neutralising various
constitutional guarantees, it moves toward a suspension of the law
[...]. The change is so significant that it disrupts the norm, and the
contraventions become the rule. The emergency procedure is substituted for the constitution and the law.'[209] 'The framework of the anti-
terrorist fight,' he adds, 'gives a new force to the Schmittian theory of
sovereignty, based on the decision regarding the emergency [...]. The
anti-terrorist fight makes the suspension of the law a foundational act
of an imperial constitution. The installation of such a juridical order
gives a new dimension to the fundamental thesis of Schmitt: the decision on the state of emergency as an act constitutive of sovereignty.
The recent anti-terrorist measures prove him right in his characterisation of the state of emergency as the enshrining of the exemption
in law. One can even say that they provide the true dimension to the
Schmittian thesis of the maintenance of the juridical order through
the decision concerning an emergency. [...] The anti-terrorist fight is
the most advanced stage in the establishment of a state of emergency
at the international level.'[210]

According to Schmitt, the separation between the exterior and
the interior normally operates through the authority of the state.

---

207 'La déstabilisation humanitaire du droit international et le retour de la "guerre juste":
une lecture critique du "Nomos de la Terre",' in *Les Etudes philosophiques*, January
2004, p. 55. Cf. also Jean-Claude Monod, *Penser l'ennemi, affronter l'exception:
Réflexions critiques sur l'actualité de Carl Schmitt* (Paris: Découverte, 2007).

208 'La déstabilisation humanitaire du droit international et le retour de la "guerre juste":
une lecture critique du "Nomos de la Terre",' p. 56.

209 'Le droit pénal comme un acte constituent: Une mutation du droit pénal,' p. 276.

210 'Le droit pénal comme un acte constituent: Une mutation du droit pénal,' pp. 282,
287-288.

Externally, the state has the possibility to make war, while internally it must establish harmony and a mode of social life regulated by law. One could say of this point of view that the interior/exterior distinction overlaps at least partially with that of norm and exception. When this distinction is abolished, the exception can also be established internally. This is what happens every time that one designates an 'internal enemy' or accuses some citizens of being accomplices of an external enemy. The state of emergency consists here in importing the logic of war, which normally prevails only on the exterior, into the interior of the society by suspending the rule of law.

But the doctrine of the state of emergency can also be used to make the politico-juridical 'normalcy' appear as a sort of continuous emergency. It is this critical dimension of the liberal legal order as the bearer of a repressed disorder or a masked repressive violence which has above all been retained by authors like Giorgio Agamben, Tonio Negri or Etienne Balibar.[211] It ends with the idea of emergency as a permanent norm: for Agamben, the government practice centred on emergency procedures has already been furtively substituted for democratic procedures and the rule of law.[212] The present state of emergency would in that case only constitute the clear revelation of an earlier latent tendency, already studied by Louis Althusser and Michel Foucault.

Nevertheless, the state of emergency loses its exceptional character when it is generalised or becomes permanent. Pierre Hassner writes that 'one distinguishes [...] tyrannical governments from others according to the way in which they use the emergency situation to render it permanent instead of seeking to return to normalcy and respect for the law.'[213] If the adoption of emergency measures by the United States appears to correspond to the Schmittian model — even while paradoxically contradicting the idea upheld by Carl Schmitt, that 'liberal' regimes are by nature incapable of dealing with the state of emergency — the fact that they are moving towards a permanent state

---

211 Cf. Jean-Claude Monod, 'La radicalité constituante (Negri, Balibar, Agamben) ou peut-on lire Schmitt de droite à gauche?,' in *Mouvements* 37, January-February 2005, pp. 80-88.

212 Cf. Giorgio Agamben, 'L'état d'exception,' in *Le Monde*, 12 December 2002; and 'Der Gewahrsam: Ausnahmezustand als Weltordnung,' in *Frankfurter Allegemeine Zeitung*, 19 April 2003.

213 *La terreur et l'empire* (Paris: Seuil, 2003), p. 200.

of emergency deviates considerably from this model. The permanence of the state of emergency — *the exception without exception* — is not Schmittian.[214] But Schmitt's thought still allows one to understand the mechanisms at work in the establishment of a permanent state of emergency; in this case a conception of hostility which smacks of theology and 'morality.' The lesson to be drawn from it is that liberal regimes are perfectly capable of taking emergency measures — but that they tend to transform the emergency into a rule under the influence of their conception of the enemy (and also, of course, of the conditions of war at a given moment). Agamben cites in this regard the prescient opinion of Walter Benjamin, according to whom 'the state of exception "in which we live" is real and absolutely cannot be distinguished from the rule.'[215] 'What, in the past, counted as an exception becomes today the normal or permanent state,' writes Robert Kurz in the same vein.[216]

---

214 Carl Schmitt has, however, been accused sometimes, notably by William B. Scheuerman and by Oren Gross ('The Normless and Exceptionless Exception: Carl Schmitt's Theory of Emergency Powers and the "Norm-Exception" Dichotomy,' in *Cardozo Law Review* XXI, 2000, pp. 1825-1867), of himself generalising the state of emergency. In certain of his writings, Schmitt would give so much importance to the emergency that the latter would end up by being substituted for the rule — just as dictatorship 'in the Roman style,' which could be only of a short duration (precisely to confront an emergency situation), can in certain circumstances be transformed into a permanent despotic power. In *Political Theology*, limited dictatorship is transformed into a sovereign dictatorship. 'What characterizes an exception,' writes Schmitt, 'is principally unlimited authority, which means the suspension of the entire existing order.' The dictator thus no longer necessarily has as as objective the reestablishment of the anterior legal order; he can also establish a new one. However, Schmitt adds at once: 'In such a situation it is clear that the state remains, whereas law recedes. Because the exception is different from anarchy and chaos, order in the juristic sense still prevails even if it is not of the ordinary kind.' (p. 12) There exists, besides, a great difference between saying that the emergency defines the norm and not vice-versa, and saying that the veritable norm is the emergency. In a kindred spirit, Marcello Montanari writes that, for Schmitt, any political circumstance whatsoever can, at the discretion of the sovereign, be declared to be 'one of emergency' ('Note sulla crisi e la critica della democrazia negli anni venti,' in Giuseppe Duso [ed.], *La politica oltre lo Stato: Carl Schmitt* [Venice: Arsenale Cooperativa, 1981], p. 159). This affirmation seems to us to be equally excessive.

215 Giorgio Agamben, *Stato di eccezione* (Torino: Bollati Boringhieri, 2003); French translation: *L'état d'exception* (Paris: Seuil, 2003, p. 144); English translation: *State of Exception* (Chicago: Chicago University Press, 2005), p. 59.

216 *Avis aux naufragés: Chroniques du capitalisme mondialisé en crise* (Paris: Lignes et Manifestes-Léo Scheer, 2005), p. 79.

4. On the Land/Sea Duality in the New 'Nomos of the Earth'

Carl Schmitt writes that 'World history is the history of the wars waged by maritime powers against land or continental powers and by land powers against sea or maritime powers.'[217] He adds that 'all important changes in history more often than not imply a new perception of space.'[218] This opposition between the land and the sea is not peculiar to him, since it is found among numerous military experts, geopoliticians and geostrategic specialists. However, for Carl Schmitt the 'logic of the land' and the 'logic of the sea' have a more extensive signification. The land is for Schmitt a historical element more than a geographical one. It is also an anthropological element: man is above all a terrestrial animal, an 'earth being.' We have seen above that Schmitt, in speaking of the partisan, attributed to him a 'telluric' character. This 'telluric' character (*das Tellurische*) is, in his work, intrinsically associated at the same time with politics, state authority and the European 'large space' (*Großraum*).[219]

The logic of land is based on spatial boundaries, that is, a division of the land into clearly distinct areas. This logic is fundamentally political, in the sense that there is no political form that is not linked to a terrestrial area — even if there are 'land' political traditions and 'maritime' traditions. The Earth determines concrete freedom, which is always a *situated* freedom, as opposed to the 'fluid' and 'formless' freedom of the sea. The Earth constitutes the substratum of thought of a concrete type. The logic of the sea is, on the contrary, intrinsically

---

217 *Land and Sea* (Washington: Plutarch Press, 1997), p. 5. The work was published for the first time in 1942: *Land und Meer: Eine weltgeschichtliche Betrachtung* (Leipzig: Reclam, 1942); latest edition: Stuttgart: Klett-Cotta, 2001); French translation: *Terre et Mer: Un point de vue sur l'histoire mondiale* (Paris: Labyrinthe, 1985), p. 23. On this problem, cf. Peter Schmidt, *Kontinentalmächte und Seemächte im weltpolitischen Denken Carl Schmitts* (Mannheim: Universität Mannheim, 1980).

218 *Land and Sea*, p. 29.

219 Cf., on this subject, Jerónimo Molina, 'Carl Schmitt y lo telúrico,' in *Razón española*, May-June 2005, pp. 263-276.

fluctuating and chaotic, for it ignores boundaries. On the sea, there are neither barriers nor borders, neither law nor property. It is in this sense that the sea can be called 'free.' As a liquid element, the sea is not subject to any state or fixed territorial sovereignty. It cannot be anyone's property for it is also the property of all: it is necessarily *res nullius* or *res omnius*.[220] That is why it is the preferred place for exchanges which operate in all directions: freedom of the seas and freedom of international commerce have constantly been associated in history. Schmitt quotes Sir Walter Raleigh, according to whom 'whoever commands the sea controls trade; whoever commands trade is master of the riches of the world.'[221] The logic of the sea is that of fluxes and refluxes.

To the land-sea distinction corresponds also a distinction between two forms of war. In the land war, '[o]nly the armies present in the field took part in the hostilities: the non-combatant, civilian population remained uninvolved in the fighting. As long as it did not take part in the battle, it was not regarded as the enemy. On the other hand, the naval wars were based on the idea of the necessity of treating the enemy's trade and economy as one. Hence the enemy was no longer the opponent in arms alone, but every inhabitant of the enemy nation, and ultimately, every neutral country that had economic links with the enemy. Land warfare implied a decisive confrontation in the field. While not excluding naval combat, the maritime war, on the other hand, favoured such characteristic means as bombardment, the blockade of the enemy shores, and the capture of enemy and neutral

---

220 Latin: 'nobody's property,' and 'everyone's (as in public) property,' concepts from ancient Roman law.-Ed.

221 (Attributed to Sir Walter Raleigh in 1640. Literally translated, the text says 'all commerce is world commerce; all world commerce is maritime commerce.'-Ed.) In his farewell address of 1796, George Washington had left these instructions: 'The great rule of conduct for us in regard to foreign nations is in extending our commercial relations, to have with them as little political connection as possible.' This is the reason why, in the course of the last two centuries, American imperialism has most often been first an economic imperialism. But Schmitt has rightly seen that the economy, when it seeks to eliminate everything that presents an obstacle to its influence, is then carried to such a level of intensity that it acquires the characteristics of politics: 'It would be more exact to say that politics continues to remain the destiny, but what has occurred is that economics has become political and thereby the destiny.' (*The Concept of Politics*, p. 78). The example of American imperialism reverses equally the old adage according to which the control of the economy goes through the conquest of territory: henceforth it is the one who controls the economy who controls the territory. Cf. *The Nomos of the Earth in the International Law of the Jus Publicum Europaeum*, Introduction.

merchantmen, by virtue of the right to capture. As such, the sea war tactics were directed both against enemy combatants and the non-combatants. Thus a starvation blockade indiscriminately affected the entire population of the involved territory: soldiers, civilians, men, women, children and old people.'[222] In *The Theory of the Partisan*, Schmitt adds that, 'Maritime war is largely trade war; it possesses quite distinctly from land war its own space and has its own concepts of enmity and spoils.'[223] Aerial bombardment of civilian populations is the modern equivalent of the blockade, which it often accompanies.

Schmitt recalls how, in the seventeenth and eighteenth centuries, ever since the Navigation Act of 1651, England took command of the oceans by attacking Spanish power and taking possession of the wealth of the Portuguese and Dutch empires. From this time, England begins a 'maritime existence.' But today, it is the United States which has replaced England as the international thalassocratic[224] power. 'It is,' says Schmitt, 'the island perfectly adapted to the times. [...] America was the larger island, through which the British mastery of the seas would be perpetuated as an Anglo-American maritime dominion of the world on a larger scale.'[225]

The famous doctrine enunciated by President James Monroe in his declaration of 2 December 1823 expressed a desire for non-intervention in European affairs, but above all the desire to make the geopolitical unit of the American continent the domain of the United States. It condemned all European intervention in any part of the American hemisphere. The Latin American countries, seeing themselves denied all national interests distinct from the interests of the United States, ceased to exist politically as a result, and tended to become mere protectorates. In 1845, the doctrine of Manifest Destiny specified that it was 'the right of [the United States'] manifest destiny to overspread and to possess the whole of the continent.'[226] The ideas

---

222 *Land and Sea*, pp. 47-48.

223 *The Theory of the Partisan*, p. 20.

224 A thalassocracy is a political power that depends primarily on its naval forces.-Ed.

225 *Land and Sea*, p. 55.

226 This comes from an article written by the journalist John L. O'Sullivan that was first published on 27 December 1845. The concept of Manifest Destiny was never officially adopted as a policy of the U.S. government, and was never universally accepted as valid, although some politicians referenced it to justify American expansionism in the mid-nineteenth century.-Ed.

inherited from these 'doctrines' would give birth to a group of principles implemented for the first time in a systematic fashion under the presidency of Theodore Roosevelt, before being extended to the world scale by Woodrow Wilson. Schmitt shows how, in the time of Wilson, what was at first only a principle of non-intervention in a given large domain — the western hemisphere — was gradually transformed into a justification for interventionism without limits. This transformation of a legitimate objective to safeguard a specific large space[227] into a universal principle that amounts to giving a quasi-religious legitimation to a particular version of imperialism marks, according to him, the beginning of the 'theologisation' of American foreign policy.[228]

The idea that the 'land' and the 'sea' are distinct entities whose confrontation can assist in understanding the history of these last centuries has been proposed by several geopoliticians, French and German as well as Anglo-Saxon. At the end of the nineteenth century, the American Alfred Thayer Mahan (1840-1914) emphasised, in two books that have remained famous,[229] the key role of the maritime factor in the consolidation of American power. He demonstrated to his compatriots that maritime power is not limited to a purely defensive military strategy, based on the protection and the security of the coastal regions, but implies the overseas extension of interests, the mastery of the seas becoming the key to a new military strategy and form the basis of a truly international power. Emphasising that the United States, already protected in the south in accordance with the Monroe Doctrine, constitutes an 'island' from the geopolitical point of view, he recalls the example of the British naval power of the seventeenth century and recommends the Americans ally themselves

227 Schmitt's original term is *Großraum*, which literally means 'large space' and is defined in his lecture 'Völkerrechtliche Grossraumprinzipien,' delivered in 1939 at Kiel University to the Nationalsozialistischen Rechtswahrer Bund (National Socialist Federation of Lawyers), as an organisational area ruled by a political idea, in this case the Reich. The term is linguistically, if not semantically, akin to the National Socialist *Lebensraum* (living space).-Tr.

228 Cf. Carl Schmitt, 'Großraum gegen Universalismus: Der völkerrechtliche Kampf um die Monroedokrin,' in *Zeitschrift der Akademie für Deutsches Recht* VI, 7, May 1939, pp. 333-337 (text reprinted in *Position und Begriffe* [Hamburg: Hanseatischer Verlagsanstalt, 1940], pp. 295-302, latest edition: Berlin: Duncker & Humblot, 1994).

229 *The Influence of Sea Power upon History, 1660-1783* (Boston: Little Brown & Co., 1890) (French translation: *Influence de la puissance maritime dans l'histoire, 1660-1783* (Paris: Claude Tchou, 2001); and *The Interest of America in Sea Power* (Boston: Little Brown & Co., 1897).

with England to contain Germany. By creating bases abroad, ensuring solid positions in the straits and on trade routes, possessing an omnipresent navy capable of acting everywhere in the world to ensure international freedom of commerce and making possible the naval blockade of enemy countries, America, predicts Mahan, can achieve world domination.[230] Following the signing of the naval disarmament treaty in 1922,[231] the United States possessed the first world battle fleet. American aero-naval power remains unmatched today.

After Mahan, the British admiral Halford J. Mackinder (1861-1947) also theorised about the confrontation of land and sea. His central thesis, defended in 1904,[232] defines the epicentre of the geopolitical phenomena on the basis of the concept of the geographic centre of the worlds. This central pivot, which he describes as the 'world island' is, in his eyes, the Eurasian continent, the heart of which consists of Germany and Russia. Mackinder advocates the idea that the essence of geopolitics is represented by the battle between the continental heartland and the extra-continental powers which surround it. This analysis would be partly repeated, but also modified, by Nicholas J. Spykman (1893-1943), especially known for having formulated the American doctrine of containment which would be applied by the United States against Russia at the beginning of the Cold War. For Spykman, the international geopolitical pivot is, however, no longer the heartland, but the rimland, the intermediary zone between the heartland and the bordering seas. In this perspective the control of the strategic zones of the Near East and Southeast Asia is of central importance.[233]

---

230 Cf. Christopher Leigh Connery, 'Ideologies of Land and Sea: Alfred Thayer Mahan, Carl Schmitt, and the Shaping of Global Myth Elements,' in *Boundary 2*, Summer 2001, pp. 173-201.

231 This was the Washington Naval Treaty, signed by the victorious powers of the First World War: the United Kingdom, the United States, Japan, France, and Italy, limiting the number and size of warships and other naval vessels that could be constructed by them. This ended up benefitting the United States enormously, since, although the Royal Navy, traditionally the world's greatest naval power, still had more warships, most of them were older, in worse condition and not as technologically advanced as the vessels of the newly-built American Navy.-Ed.

232 Halford J. Mackinder propounded his doctrine for the first time during a speech ('The Geographical Pivot of History') made on 25 January 1904 before the Royal Geographical Society of London.

233 Cf. Aymeric Chauprade, *Géopolitique: Constantes et changements dans l'histoire* (Paris: Ellipses, 2001).

With the advent of aviation, a new element has been added to the land and the sea: air. Schmitt has rightly noted the growing importance of the air, in which he sees the future: 'Since World War I airspace has been added as a new dimension, altering both the old theaters of land and sea in their spatial structure.'[234] In *Land and Sea*, he defines air as a 'the new elemental space of human existence.'[235] In fact, taking a closer look, air has many points in common with the sea. Its principal characteristics are extent, ubiquity, emptiness and fluidity: not being subjected to any 'allegiance,' air space favours rapid movement from one point to another on the face of the Earth. Other features it shares with the sea is that it is not a space subjected to borders, in the classical sense of the term, that it is a medium of transport and communication, and, finally, that it constitutes an instrument for the projection of strength and power.

Air is today one of the determining elements of military strategy, but also of terrorist action. The strategic use of outer space, which is not a simple extension of air space, has also already started. It is used for strictly military purposes (identification and localisation of targets, tapping, observation and surveillance, etc.) as well as for intelligence, telecommunication, meteorology, spying, and so on. The chief characteristics of outer space are vastness, hyper-altitude, emptiness and (relative) invulnerability. Its military use through spacecraft should, in the long run, permit not only new offensive strategies but also bring about a radical transformation of the use of land forces, space being destined to establish itself as the preferred medium for the informational dimension of operations.[236]

The United States already considers space a potential strategic theatre, meaning that supremacy in space is already part of their military objectives. Since the time of the Cold War, the United States has devoted ever-larger resources to achieving the mastery of space. In its plan, space is not only considered as a multiplier of power, but as a weapon in itself. This is borne out by its project of a space-based anti-missile defence, revived in December 2002 by George W. Bush,

---

234 *The Theory of the Partisan*, p. 48.

235 *Land and Sea*, p. 58.

236 On the role of space and, more especially, of outer space in present-day strategic thought, cf. Serge Grouard, *La guerre en orbite: Essai de politique et de stratégie spatiales* (Paris: Economica-FEDN, 1994); and Benoît d'Albion, 'L'emploi des armes aériennes dans les conflits modernes,' in *Revue de défense nationale*, January 1996.

an idea inherited from the 'Star Wars' concept of the Reagan admin-istration, which has as its principal strategic goal not only the capacity to intercept intercontinental ballistic missiles but also the deployment in orbital space of laser batteries, the purpose of which is to endow America with the capacity to carry out preventive strikes of a new type. It is equally significant that the Pentagon envisages that its over-seas bases will decrease in importance, as certain functions could potentially be taken over by spacecraft.[237] One may thus wonder, writes Christian Malis, 'if space is not destined to play a role analo-gous to that of the sea in the Mackinderian geopolitics.' 'If the oceans,' he adds, 'have for a long time constituted the preferred mode of sup-port for the United States and the protective space for its conquering industrial economy, doubtless space is destined to join the sea to sup-port and protect an economy based also on information.'[238]

After 1945, the essential theme of the writings of Schmitt is that of the '*nomos* of the Earth.' According to Schmitt, the modern age signifies the disappearance of the old *nomos*, and he investigates what is destined to succeed it. One of the essential questions he poses is whether history is oriented towards a political unification of the world and what the consequences of that would be, both for the world and for the concept of politics itself.

---

237 Cf., on this subject, Thierry Garcin, 'L'espace, outil géopolitique des Etats-Unis,' in Aymeric Chauprade (ed.), *Géopolitique des Etats-Unis: Culture, intérêts, stratégies* (Paris: Ellipses, 2004), pp. 69-74, who emphasises that 'the American will to exercise a predominance or hegemony based in part on space is [equally] evident in the civil domain, beginning with the terrestrial network of receiving stations' (p. 72). On 6 October 2006, the White House published a new document on its space policy (National Space Policy). The text emphasises that 'United States national security is critically dependent upon space capabilities, and this dependence will grow,' is opposed to any treaty prohibiting space arms ('The United States considers space capabilities [...] vital to its national interests. [...] The United States will oppose the development of new legal regimes or other restrictions that seek to prohibit or limit U.S. access to or use of space') and specifies that the United States will 'deny, if necessary, adversaries the use of space capabilities hostile to U.S. national interests.' Cf. also Peter Hayes (ed.), *Space Power Interests* (Boulder: Westview Press, 1996); Jean-Michel Valantin, 'Militarisation de l'espace et puissance américaine,' in *Diplomatie*, January-February 2003, pp. 50-52; and Eduardo Mendieta, 'War the School of Space: The Space of War and the War for Space,' in *Ethics, Place and Environment* IX, 2, June 2006, pp. 207-229, who compares the geostrategic thought of Carl Schmitt with those of Friedrich Ratzel, A. T. Mahan, Halford Mackinder and Guilio Duohet.

238 'L'espace extra-atmosphérique, enjeu stratégique et conflictualité de demain,' text available at www.stratisc.org.

As we have seen, Schmitt contends that from 1890 the old Westphalian order of the *jus publicum europaeum*, born at the end of the Thirty Years' War (1648), began to dissolve into a 'universalism without territories' and into the 'empty' and abstract normativism of an international legality on which no accord can be established, abandoning its European centring without succeeding in finding a substitute basis of legitimacy. Carl Schmitt gives, in this perspective, a central place to the Treaty of Versailles, which not only pulled down Germany and substituted the principle of nationalities for the legitimacy of the ancient dynasties but also represented the moment when Europe found itself truly dethroned from its old prerogatives.[239]

Schmitt sees in the *nomos* of the earth — a term he used for the first time in 1934, when he partly abandoned his old decisionism to instead rally to a 'thought of concrete order' (*konkretes Ordnungsdenken*) giving a significant role to the institutionalism of Maurice Hauriou and Santi Romano — an ordered group of political entities linked by common rules. The *nomos* is not understood in his works in the sense of a law (*Gesetz*), that is to say, as a simple product of legislation, but as a 'first measure' (*Messung*), an original distribution or sharing of space. The error of Western modernity, according to Schmitt, has been to replace the law as concrete order (*nomos*) with the law as a simple rule (*Gesetz*). *Nomos* is of course related to the logic of the Earth, to the extent that everything in it is a matter of boundaries. Without boundaries, without spatial limits, no order is possible: every fundamental order (*Grundordnung*) is a spatial order (*Raumordnung*). Law itself, emphasises Schmitt, has a telluric foundation 'in which space and law, order and orientation meet.'[240] From concrete thought's point of view, every *nomos* results from a unity of spatial order (*Ordnung*) and orientation (*Ordnung*), i.e., from the possibility of orienting oneself within the world of a given community. *Nomos*, finally, is the immediate form

---

239 Cf. Carl Schmitt, 'Die Auflösung der europäischen Ordnung im "International Law," 1890-1939,' in *Deutsche Rechtswissenschaft* V, 4, 9 November 1940, pp. 267-278 (text reprinted in Günter Maschke (ed.), *Staat, Großraum, Nomos: Arbeiten aus den Jahren 1916-1969* [Berlin: Duncker & Humblot, 1995], pp. 372-387). 'The replacement of a single, Eurocentric, public law-governed system of sovereignties by private law relations governing a global free market and the establishment of a morally-based imperial order that knows war only as a relationship between the police and the criminal have rarely been analysed with a sharper eye,' writes Martti Koskenniemi ('International Law as Political Theology: How to Read *Nomos der Erde*?,' in *Constellations* XI, 2004, 4, p. 500).

240 *The Nomos of the Earth*, p. 47.

(*unmittelbare Gestalt*) through which the social and political order of
a people becomes spatially visible. Insofar as it constitutes a concrete
territorial and spatial order, the *nomos* represents the overall order of
the Earth.

The question of the 'new *nomos* of the Earth' arises in the form of
an alternative, which Carl Schmitt defined already in the late 1930s:
the world of the future will be either unipolar or multipolar. If it is
unipolar, it will inevitably be subjected to the hegemony of the dominant power, which can today be only the United States. That will then
be the advent of a unified world that Schmitt equates with the end
of politics, since the essence of politics implies that one can always
determine, in relation to the plurality of actors, who is the friend and
who the enemy (there is politics only as long as there exist at least two
different polities). If, on the contrary, the world remains a 'political'
world, it will quite necessarily also be a multipolar world, composed
of 'large spaces' (*Großräume*) — cultural territories and crucibles of
civilisation, but also of geopolitical territories — which alone will be
able to play a role of regulation and diversification in relation to the
vast movement of globalisation. Schmitt summarises this alternative
in the formula: 'Large space against universalism.'[241]

Carl Schmitt first set out his views on the 'large space' (*Großraum*)
in a small book which appeared in 1939 containing the text of a lecture

---

241 '*Großraum gegen Universalismus.*' Perhaps it should nevertheless be emphasised
that the 'universalism' of which the Catholic Carl Schmitt speaks is not just any
universalism but what he himself calls a 'false universalism,' essentiallly nihilist. On
this point, cf. Martti Koskenniemi, 'International Law as Political Theology: How to
Read *Nomos der Erde*?,' who thinks that, in Schmitt, this 'false universalism' is
opposed to a universalism based on faith. The translation into English of the *Nomos
der Erde* has besides already opened a debate in the Anglo-Saxon countries. Cf.
Mitchell Dean, '*Nomos* and the Politics of World Order,' in Larner &. Walters (eds.),
Global Governmentality (London: Routledge, 2004); Mika Ojakangas, 'A Terrifying
World without an Exterior: Carl Schmitt and the Metaphysics of International (Dis)
Order,' paper at the colloquium 'The International Thought of Carl Schmitt,' The
Hague, 9-11 September 2004; Alzbeta Dufferová, 'The Historical Thinking of Carl
Schmitt and its Signification for the World Orders,' paper at the same colloquium;
World Orders: Confronting Carl Schmitt's The Nomos of the Earth, special issue of
the journal *The South Atlantic Quarterly*, Spring 2005, pp. 177-392; Christoph
Burchard, 'Interlinking the Domestic with the International: Carl Schmitt on
Democracy and International Relations,' in *Leiden Journal of International Law* XIX,
2006, 1, pp. 9-40; and Thalin Zarmanian, 'Carl Schmitt and the Problem of Legal
Order: From Domestic to International,' ibid., pp. 41-67.

delivered the same year in Kiel.[242] In the 'large space,' he does not hesitate to see a new category of the science of international law, and he emphasises explicitly that this category, which he presents as a 'concrete, historical and politically contemporary concept' (*'konkreten geschichtlich-politischen Gegenwartsbegriff'*)[243] is destined to take the place of the old nation-state order which entered a crisis already in the 1930s and has now become obsolete.[244] The 'large spaces,' adds Schmitt — and that is the most important point — must ensure their autonomy and their freedom of movement by adopting, as the United States has done with the Monroe Doctrine, a 'doctrine' prohibiting all intervention of foreign powers in the territory that is not their own.[245]

---

242 *Völkerrechtliche Großraumordnung mit Interventionsverbot für raumfremde Mächte: Ein Beitrag zum Reichsbegriff im Völkerrecht* (Berlin-Vienna-Leipzig: Deutscher Rechtsverlag, 1939). The work went through four successive editions between 1939 and 1942, with revisions each time. It was republished in the collection published under the direction of Günter Maschke, *Staat, Großraum, Nomos*, pp. 269-371. In the Third Reich, it was the object of violent critiques on the part of certain Nazi jurists or theoreticians, notably Werner Best, Reinhard Höhn and Wilhelm Stuckart. Cf. also Joseph H. Kaiser, 'Europäiches Großraumdenken: Die Steigerung geschichtlicher Größen als Rechtsproblem,' in Hans Barion, Ernst Wolfgang Böckenförde, Ernst Forsthoff and E. Weber (eds.), *Epirrhosis: Festgabe für Carl Schmitt* (Berlin: Duncker & Humblot, 1968), vol. 2, pp. 319-331; Matthias Schmoeckel, *Die Großraumtheorie: Ein Beitrag zur Geschichte der Völkerrechtswissenschaft im Dritten Reich, insbesondere der Kriegszeit* (Berlin: Duncker & Humblot, 1994). On the present-day strategic aspects of the concept of the large space, cf. Adolfo Sergio Spadoni, *Nomos e tecnica: Ragion strategica e pensiero filosofico-giuridico nell'Ordinamento dei grandi spazi* (Naples: Edizione Scientifiche italiane, 2005), principally Chapter 1, 'Dall'idrosofia alla cosmosofia: Considerazioni sul "Großraumdenken" di Carl Schmitt,' pp. 11-70).

243 From *Völkerrechtliche Großraumordnung mit Interventionsverbot für raumfremde Mächte*, p. 305, cited in Christian Joerges and Navraj Singh Ghaleigh, *Darker Legacies of Law in Europe: The Shadow of National Socialism and Fascism over Europe and Its Legal Traditions* (Oxford: Hart, 2003), p. 177.-Ed.

244 Schmitt declares in 1932, 'The era of the state is in its decline. [...] The state, the model of political unity, and invested with the most stunning monopoly of all, that of political decision, the state, this masterpiece of the European form and Western rationalism, has been dethroned' (*La notion de politique*, pp. 42-43). Although he himself was profoundly a statist, Schmitt took care never to confuse state and politics. The antithesis of friend and enemy, which is, according to him, the foundation of politics, is historically and ontologically anterior to the appearance of the state. Inversely, when politics abandons its classical authority, the state authority, it is only to manifest itself under other forms and by other means. The nation-state, in other words, is only a political entity among other possible ones. State and politics have for a long time been superimposed on each other but have never been confused.

245 In his book, Carl Schmitt retraces the way in which, from the moment when the Monroe Doctrine was proclaimed, the United States has constantly claimed, to its benefit, a right of intervention permitting it to posit itself as 'arbitrator of the Earth.'

At the same time that he substitutes the 'large space' for the State, Schmitt predicts a corresponding transition from the notion of *territory*, the corollary of the classic concept of the nation-state, to that of a *space*[246] with flexible limits, not determined in advance. Provided with aerial as well as terrestrial or maritime dimensions, a 'space' is not simply a larger territory. Whereas territory is a state notion, space corresponds to a dynamic reality. As Jean-François Kervégan writes, 'The shift from the problem of the closed territory and the state to that of the large space and imperial power reflects, according to Schmitt, the expiration of the legal and political order of modern Europe. The development of the totalitarian state was the precursor of this expiration.'[247] But Schmitt also allots a new and significant role to the notion of empire (*Reich*) which, in history, long represented the chief alternative to the model of the nation-state. He considers that each 'large space' should be centred on an empire, which would regulate the relations of the member countries and permit the 'large space' to develop its own particular politics. But he emphasises also that the *Großraum* should not be confused with the *Reich*, whose mission is only to organise the 'large space' and protect it from foreign intrusion. Finally, he admits that 'empires,' and no longer nations, could indeed become the principal actors of international relations, even while warning against a simple, mechanical extension of the idea of national sovereignty to the scale of the '*Großraum*.'[248]

The question of whether the European Union of today constitutes a 'large space' in the sense that Carl Schmitt uses the term, or if one can establish a relation between the views of Schmitt and one or the other form of the federalist doctrine, has recently been discussed on several occasions.[249] Such discussions always contain a fair amount

---

According to him, the United States has dominated international law since 1919, and this procedure culminated at the moment of the Kellogg-Briand Pact of 1928.

246 The *Raum* in the term *Großraum*, here taken in its literal sense.-Tr.

247 'Carl Schmitt et "l'unité du monde",' p. 13.

248 On the way in which Carl Schmitt establishes a link between domain and empire, cf. also his text of 1951, 'Raum und Rom: Zur Phonetik des Wortes Raum,' in *Universitas* VI, 9, September 1951, pp. 963-968 (text reprinted in *Staat, Großraum, Nomos*, pp. 491-495), where he indulges in a connection between the German term for space, *Raum*, and the name of the city of Rome.

249 Cf., notably, Olivier Beaud, 'Fédéralisme et souveraineté, notes pour une théorie constitutionnelle de la Fédération,' in *Revue de droit public*, 1998, 1, pp. 86 ff.; Jerónimo Molina, '¿Unión europea o gran espacio?,' in *Razón española*, September-October 2002, pp. 161-182; Constantin Houchard, *Carl Schmitt, la Fédération et*

of speculation insofar as Schmitt, even though he died in 1985, almost thirty years after the Treaty of Rome was signed, never published anything on the nature of the European Community. Certain authors who want to make Europe an autonomous power, notably in matters of foreign policy and defence, have explicitly referred to the Schmittian model of the 'large space' and to his idea of a new *nomos* of the Earth,[250] and even to the idea of empire in opposition to that of the nation-state. On the other hand, certain adversaries of the European construct have sought to justify their opposition to this project with reference to the views developed by Schmitt, which they have sought to present in the worst possible light.[251]

l'Union européenne, Seminar on General State Theory and History of Political Ideas, Catholic University of Leuven, Louvain-la-Neuve 2002. The thesis, according to which the constitutional court of federal Germany based its judgment regarding the Maastricht Treaty on criteria relating to a Schmittian conception of democracy, has been supported by Joseph H. Weiler, 'Does Europe Need a Constitution? *Demos, Telos*, and the German Decision,' in *European Law Journal*, 1995, 1, pp. 219 ff. (cf. also, by the same author, 'The State "*über alles*": *Demos, Telos* and the German Decision,' in Ole Due, Marcus Lutter and Jürgen Schwarze, eds., *Festschrift für Ulrich Everling* (Baden-Baden: Nomos, 1995), vol. 2, pp. 1651 ff.). This thesis has been the object of a critical examination: Peter L. Lindseth, *The Maastricht Decision Ten Years Later: Parliamentary Democracy, Separation of Powers, and the Schmittian Interpretation Reconsidered*, European University Institute, San Domenico di Fiesole 2003.

250 Cf., for example, Carlo Masala, 'Europa sollte ein Reich werden: Carl Schmitts Großraumtheorie könnte helfen, dem imperialen Universalismus der Vereinigten Staaten auf kluge Weise zu entkommen,' in *Frankfurter Allgemeine Zeitung*, 10 October 2004, p. 15. Cf. also Carmelo Jiménez Segado, 'Carl Schmitt and the "Grossraum" of the "Reich": A revival of the Idea of Empire,' paper at the colloquium 'The International Thought of Carl Schmitt,' The Hague, 9-11 September 2004.

251 John Laughland, the great adversary of the European construct, has published a polemical book (*The Tainted Source: The Undemocratic Origins of the European Idea* [London: Warner, 1997]) in which he relates this project to the ideas of Carl Schmitt on the subject of the 'large space,' by systematically confusing these ideas with the Nazi plans for the organisation and rearrangement of Europe. The work, which in fact strives to reconnect the project of European construction to the idea that the Nazis had for the future Europe, was the object of a reply as well as a clarification: Alexander Proelß, 'Nationalsozialistische Baupläne für das europäische Haus? John Laughland's "The Tainted Source" vor dem Hintergrund der Großraumtheorie Carl Schmitts,' in *Forum historiae juris*, 12 May 2003. Proelß shows in what the concept of *Großraum* in Schmitt is radically different from the conception of the European territory as it was expounded in the 1940s by SS theoreticians like Werner Best or Reinhard Höhn, who systematically opposed the idea of *völkische Großraumordnung* (rule of the large space according to its *Volk*) to that of *völkerrechtliche Großraumordnung* (rule of the large space according to international law). The same subject gave rise on 29-30 September 2000 to a colloquium at the European University Institute of Florence, whose proceedings have been published: Christian Joerges and Navraj Singh Ghaleigh (eds.), *Darker*

Carl Schmitt addresses the question of federation (*Bund*) only in chapters 29 and 30 of his *Constitutional Theory* of 1928.[252] His definition of the federation does not confuse the concept with the classical federal state (*Bundesstaat*), nor with the confederal state or confederation of states (*Staatenbund*). The federation, he writes, 'is a durable union based on a free convention, serving the common aim of the political conservation of all the members of the federation; it modifies the global political *status* of each member of the federation according to this common aim.'[253] The entry into a federation thus brings about for the states a modification of their constitutions. The federative pact (*Bundesvertrag*) is an 'inter-state statutory pact'[254] whose ratification represents an act of constitutional power. Every federation possesses as such a political existence corresponding to a *jus belli* which is its own. It is at the same time a subject of international law and a subject of internal law. Schmitt emphasises also the paradoxes or the antinomies of a federation. One of the most obvious is that the member states normally subscribe to the federative pact in order to preserve their political autonomy whereas, by entering into the federation, they must abandon a part of it.[255] But the most important is this: 'A federation juxtaposes two types of political existence: the global existence of the federation and the particular existence of the member state. [...] On both sides, gradations are possible, but the extreme case always

Legacies of Law in Europe: The Shadow of National Socialism and Fascism over Europe and its Legal Traditions. One should read especially the papers of Navraj Singh Ghaleigh ('"Looking into the Brightly Lit Room": Braving Carl Schmitt in "Europe",' pp. 43-54), John P. McCormick ('Carl Schmitt's Europe. Cultural: Imperial and Spatial Proposals for European Integration, 1923-1955,' pp. 133-141), Christian Joerges ('Europe a "Großraum"? Shifting Legal Conceptualisations of the Integration Project,' pp. 167-191) and Neil Walker ('From "Großraum" to Condominium: A Comment,' pp. 193-203). On the project of European construction, cf. also Ben Rosamond, *Theories of European Integration* (Basingstoke: Macmillan, 2000); and Dimitris N. Chryssochoou, *Theorizing European Integration* (London: Sage, 2001).

252 *Verfassungslehre* (Munich-Leipzig: Duncker & Humblot, 1928); latest edition: Berlin 2003; French translation: *Théorie de la Constitution* (Paris: Presses universitaires de France, 1993). These passages have been translated into English, with a commentary, by Gary L. Ulmen: 'The Constitutional Theory of Federation,' in *Telos* 91, Spring 1992, pp. 26–56. Full English translation: *Constitutional Theory* (Durham: Duke University Press, 2008).

253 *Théorie de la Constitution*, p. 512.

254 *Théorie de la Constitution*, p. 513.

255 'The federal right always prevails over the right of the member state insofar as the federation acts within the framework of its authority vis-à-vis the member states' (*Théorie de la Constitution*, p. 529).

leads either to the dissolution of the federation which then leaves on the scene only isolated states, or to the disappearance of the member states, which then lets only a sole state survive.'[256] These antinomies can be resolved, adds Schmitt, only if there is a substantial homogeneity among the members of the federation, this homogeneity alone being able to establish a concrete accord (*Übereinstimmung*) among them.

With the concept of the 'large space' to which Schmitt explicitly opposes that of 'universalism,' there appears in any case an alternative of more recent date: the unity or the plurality of the world. Will there be a universe or a 'pluriverse,' a homogeneous globalisation or a globalisation that respects the diversity of cultures and peoples? Schmitt shows that the old order, which was that of modernity, can no longer be Eurocentric, but implies in the postmodern era a general rearrangement of international relations around a simple alternative: unipolarity or multipolarity. Unipolarity, which one could call 'monotheistic,' sanctions the hegemony of the dominant power; multipolarity, in keeping with the 'polytheism of values' (Max Weber)[257] is based on the mutual recognition of politico-cultural groups of equal value. 'The development of the planet,' writes Schmitt, has 'reached a clear dilemma between universalism and pluralism, between monopoly and polypoly. The question was whether the planet was mature enough for a global monopoly of a single power or whether a pluralism of coexisting *Großräume*, spheres of influence, and cultural spheres would determine the new international law of the earth.'[258]

Schmitt does not hide his preference for the coexistence of '[a] combination of several independent *Großräume* or blocs [which] could constitute a balance, and thereby could precipitate a new order of the earth.'[259] From the 1950s, he foresees that the binary division of the world inherited from Yalta, between the 'free world' and the Soviet bloc, does not herald so much the unification of the world as a 'transition to a new plurality.' Europe remains for him the territorial

---

256 *Théorie de la Constitution*, p. 518.

257 In *The Protestant Ethic in the Spirit of Capitalism*, Max Weber coins the term 'polytheism of values' to describe the multiple forms of truth that have arisen in modern times to replace the absolute truths that were offered by religion and other traditional forms in previous eras.-Ed.

258 *The Nomos of the Earth*, p. 243-244.

259 *The Nomos of the Earth*, p. 355.

space 'in which the geo-political arrangement most conducive to world peace developed.'[260]

The alternative between the unipolar world and the multipolar world corresponds to the opposition between sea and land, for a multipolar world implies the territorial concept of borders. In today's world, land logic more than ever coincides with a continental logic, that of the whole of Europe (or of Eurasia), whereas maritime logic, incarnated formerly by England, is today that of America. Likewise, one could say, the alternatives of a European Union as a simple trans-atlantic domain of free trade and a European Union as an autonomous continental power relates again to this opposition, to the extent that the sea is on the side of commerce whereas the land is essentially on the side of politics. That is, indeed, why the United States so frequently expresses its adherence to the unipolar model, which would sanction its planetary hegemony. Already in 1991, Charles Krauthammer wrote, 'We are living in a unipolar world. We Americans should like it — and exploit it.'[261] 'The Americans,' Thierry de Montbrial declares, 'reject categorically the concept of a multipolar world, whose two constituents are unacceptable in their eyes. On the one hand, who-ever says multipolar implies a balance of powers and thus precisely the necessity for a counterweight to the United States. [...] It does not accept, on the other hand, having any balance guaranteed by the United Nations, that is, practically by the Security Council and, more precisely, by its five permanent members.'[262]

Consequently, the major geopolitical objective of the United States is to avoid the formation of a continental or Eurasian heartland which could rival its own power, that is, to do everything to avoid the emer-gence of a rival power in Western Europe, in Asia or on the territory of the former Russian Empire. Hence the redefinition of the missions of NATO and the enlargement of its strategic objectives, although this organisation, which was in the beginning purely defensive, has lost its *raison d'être* after the collapse of the Soviet system. The growing importance of the Pacific Ocean in the affairs of the world and the

---

260 John P. McCormick, 'Carl Schmitt's Europe: Cultural, Imperial and Spatial Proposals for European Integration, 1923-1955.'

261 *The Washington Post*, 22 March 1991

262 *La guerre et la diversité du monde: Les Etats-Unis contre l'Europe puissance* (La Tour d'Aigues: L'Aube, 2004), p. 120.

fact that the United States is looking more and more in that direction go hand in hand.

Insofar as it is characterised by the proliferation of networks and flows of all sorts (commercial, financial, technological, communication, etc.), globalisation too is related to the logic of the sea, which does not recognise any borders or closed territories. By a habit of speech which is itself revealing, one says that globalisation unifies the Earth, but in fact by unifying it, it subjects the Earth to the logic of the sea, which is that of the abolition of borders and the supremacy of fluxes and refluxes.

After having put an end to international bipolarity, globalisation brings about a generalised deterritorialisation of military, political, economic and financial relations. Abolishing territorial space, it also abolishes temporality by establishing a 'zero hour' due to its ubiquity and instantaneity. With the internationalisation of capitalism, just as with global neo-terrorism, one again enters into the 'smooth space' that Gilles Deleuze and Félix Guattari formerly opposed to 'grooved space.' Whereas 'grooved space' is thought of on the model of tissue, with its structure, fabric and finitude, 'smooth space' is conceived on the model of felt, which involves no friction or any meshing, but only a tangle of homogenous fibres which can grow infinitely in all directions. 'Smooth' space is not situated, but 'nomadic'; a space without depth, a space of immediacy and contact in all directions, containing neither forms nor subjects, but only flux without anchoring or polarisation. '[A]t the complementary and dominant level of an integrated (or rather integrating) world capitalism,' write Deleuze and Guattari, 'a new smooth space is produced in which capital reaches its "absolute" speed. [...] The multinationals fabricate a kind of deterritorialized smooth space in which points of occupation as well as poles of exchange become quite independent of the classical paths to striation.'[263]

---

263 Gilles Deleuze and Félix Guattari, *A Thousand Plateaus: Capitalism and Schizophrenia* (Minneapolis: The University of Minnesota Press), p. 492. 'One may wonder,' comments Mireille Buydens, 'if the smooth is not a useful model for thinking of financial post-capitalism, whose fluxes centre, recede or glide, and are displaced and clustered around values according to "laws" that have more affinity with the mysterious necessities of storm meteorology than with predictive science' ('Espace lisse/Espace strié,' in Robert Sasso and Arnaud Villani, eds., *Le vocabulaire de Gilles Deleuze*, special issue of the *Cahiers de Noesis*, 3, Spring 2003, p. 135).

In his diary, Carl Schmitt expressed his horror at the scenario which Paul Virilio has called 'globalitarianism,' that is, the future of a globalised world which, by definition, would be a world without an exterior and thus without the possibility of politics: 'How frightful it is, the world where there is nothing external, but only the interior.'[264] The same sentiment is found in Schmitt's works. In *The Concept of the Political*, for example, Schmitt expresses several times his fear that there may arise a 'completely pacified globe,' which 'would be a world without the distinction of friend and enemy and hence a world without politics.'[265] The 'creation of an alliance of nations encompassing the whole of humanity,' the advent of a world state or a universal society, he thinks, 'mean total depoliticalization.'[266] Schmitt even says explicitly that perhaps there will exist one day a totally depoliticised state of humanity, contenting himself with adding that 'in the meantime it does not exist.'[267]

This fear is quite strange considering his definition of politics itself—the more so in that Carl Schmitt also says that a unified world would be a world where wars would not disappear, but would all resemble civil wars. If, in fact, politics 'does not designate its own proper domain, but only the degree of intensity of an association or dissociation of human beings,'[268] if it can 'draw its strength from the most different fields of life,' if 'every imaginable domain of human activity is potentially political and becomes immediately political when the fundamental conflicts and fundamental questions are transported into this field,'[269] then it is difficult to see how politics could disappear—and what is the basis for Schmitt's pessimism, or at least unease. If politics is indeed what Schmitt says it is, that is, a characteristic dimension of human existence, and if every conflict, no matter what its nature, automatically becomes political as soon as it attains a certain degree of intensity, one should rather arrive at the conclusion that politics is permanent and inevitable: 'Man would

264 *Glossarium: Aufzeichnungen der Jahre 1947-1951* (Berlin: Duncker & Humblot, 1991), for 5 November 1947.

265 *The Concept of the Political*, p. 35.

266 *The Concept of the Political*, p. 55.

267 *La notion de politique*, p. 18.

268 *The Concept of the Political*, p. 38.

269 *Der Hüter der Verfassung*, J. C. B. Mohr-Paul Siebeck, Tübingen 1931 (latest edition: Duncker u. Humblot, Berlin 1996), p. 111.

cease to be man if he ceased to be political.'[270] Globalisation is thus not synonymous with the end of politics, and all the less so in that the tendency towards the unification of the world brings, as a reaction and in a symmetrical manner, new fragmentations or divisions into its midst. A globalised world is not necessarily a pacified world, quite the contrary. Even though he clearly distinguishes the state from politics and was one of the first to recognise the disintegration of the nation-state of the classic type, Carl Schmitt has perhaps quite simply found it difficult to imagine positive non-state forms of political life.

At the end of this survey we arrive at the following conclusion. George W. Bush and his entourage are clearly not 'Schmittian' political men. Masters of the power of the sea, they appeal to a political and ideological model that Schmitt always criticised. Their liberalism (in the European sense of the term) and their messianic optimism are as alien to Schmitt's ideas as the manner in which they conceive of war as a 'just' war, where the enemy is never recognised, but designated as a figure of evil who should be eradicated, or in which they use the concept of the emergency to establish a permanent state of emergency. On the other hand, it is undeniable that, owing to the politics initiated some years ago by the American administration, some properly Schmittian themes have returned to the foreground of international affairs and that these themes are so many hermeneutic keys that can help us understand what is happening. We hope to have shown here both the topicality of the principal themes of the thought of Carl Schmitt and the inanity of the notion according to which the American neoconservatives are considered to be faithful disciples of his thought.

---

270 S. Parvez Manzoor, 'The Sovereignty of the Political: Carl Schmitt and the Nemesis of Liberalism,' in *The Muslim World Book Review*, Autumn 1999.

Other titles published by Arktos:

Beyond Human Rights
by Alain de Benoist

Manifesto for a European Renaissance
by Alain de Benoist & Charles Champetier

The Problem of Democracy
by Alain de Benoist

Germany's Third Empire
by Arthur Moeller van den Bruck

The Arctic Home in the Vedas
by Bal Gangadhar Tilak

Revolution from Above
by Kerry Bolton

The Fourth Political Theory
by Alexander Dugin

Hare Krishna in the Modern World
by Graham Dwyer & Richard J. Cole

Fascism Viewed from the Right
by Julius Evola

Metaphysics of War
by Julius Evola

Notes on the Third Reich
by Julius Evola

The Path of Cinnabar
by Julius Evola

Archeofuturism
by Guillaume Faye

Convergence of Catastrophes
by Guillaume Faye

Why We Fight
by Guillaume Faye

The WASP Question
by Andrew Fraser

War and Democracy
by Paul Gottfried

The Saga of the Aryan Race
by Porus Homi Havewala

Homo Maximus
by Lars Holger Holm

The Owls of Afrasiab
by Lars Holger Holm

De Naturae Natura
by Alexander Jacob

Fighting for the Essence
by Pierre Krebs

Can Life Prevail?
by Pentti Linkola

Guillaume Faye and the Battle of Europe
by Michael O'Meara

New Culture, New Right
by Michael O'Meara

The Ten Commandments of Propaganda
by Brian Anse Patrick

Morning Crafts
by Tito Perdue

A Handbook of Traditional Living
by Raido

The Agni and the Ecstasy
by Steven J. Rosen

The Jedi in the Lotus
by Steven J. Rosen

It Cannot Be Stormed
by Ernst von Salomon

The Outlaws
by Ernst von Salomon

Tradition & Revolution
by Troy Southgate

Against Democracy and Equality
by Tomislav Sunic

Generation Identity
by Markus Willinger

The Initiate: Journal of Traditional Studies
by David J. Wingfield (ed.)

Lightning Source UK Ltd.
Milton Keynes UK
UKOW04f2058191214

243456UK00001B/83/P